Courtesy of Olympic National Park

Courtesy of Olympic National Park

Courtesy of Olympic National Park

Courtesy of Olympic National Park

Hibben and Bole photo

Courtesy of Marilyn Lewis

Courtesy of Marilyn Lewis

Courtesy of Marilyn Lewis

HIGH DIVIDE

First Edition, 2005

Printed by:
Olympic Graphic Arts, Inc.
640 S. Forks Ave.
Forks, WA 98331

ISBN 0-615-13006-2

Published by:
POSEIDON PEAK PUBLISHING
4913 Upper Hoh Road
Forks, WA 98331

To order: 360-374-5254 TOLL FREE: 1-866-457-8398 FAX: 360-374-5266
Email: glynda@olypen.com

CREDITS:
Cover illustration and design: Jack Datisman
Negatives: Chuck Cantellay
Photo restoration and publication layout: Trevor Henry

Photos: Peterson Family collection
           Ruth Kirk
           Marilyn Lewis
           Cougar Fields
           Hibben and Bole collection
           Olympic National Park
           Olympic National Forest
           Clallam County Sheriff's Dept.

Contents

DEDICATION

What were the stories behind this scenery and who shaped and were shaped by this landscape? A cross section of America came to Sol Duc in its glory years, from the cultural elites of the day to pop icons to flimflam men and all manner of humanity between. This book is dedicated to them.

There was Chris Morganroth, the German emegré who homesteaded the Upper Bogachiel, whose first wife was a Quillayute, who became the first District Ranger of the Olympic National Forest and who was midwife to the birth of the Olympic National Park.

There were the academics C. J. Albrecht and Pat Bole, who thrilled eastern audiences with their tales of adventure and exploration in the West.

There was also Dr. Frank C. Hibben, professor, author, lecturer and philanthropist, outdoor adventurer and secret agent for the US Government and original adrenalin junkie.

There was Tom Newton, mountain man.

There were District Ranger Sanford Floe and his wife, Esther, who loved the mountains as much as Minnie.

There was Maynard Fields, the forest guard at Bogachiel Peak and Maynard's intended, Claudia, who worked the counter at Sol Duc.

There were Rangers Buckmaster and VanDevanter at the Eagle Station who kept tourists on the straight and narrow.

There was beautiful actress, Francis Farmer, who came to Sol Duc just to find peace and whose demons patiently waited for her back in Seattle.

There was Howard Hughes, tycoon and visionary, who never saw Sol Duc but needed its timber to make his monster flying boat.

There was Micky Merchant, an early snowbird who spent his winters prospecting and cowboying in the Southwest and who would follow Minnie through hell and high water and often did.

There was US Supreme Court Justice William O. Douglas, outdoorsman and womanizer, in a league of his own in both fields.

There was the free spirit, Evelyn Estes, who rode her horse from Tennessee to California and wound up at Sol Duc in the early forties and who worshipped the ground Minnie walked on.

There was George Brown, who at fourteen pleaded in a letter for a job with Minnie, and who thirty years later made the same plea for his son.

There was Martel Gilbert, Minnie's helper in the early fifties, who later headed the drama department at Chico State in California.

There was the local girl, Marge McClean.

There was Ann St. John, the fifties beatnik and budding anarchist/communist whose dad had been killed in a Lake Crescent area mine accident, who had the courage of her convictions and subsequently moved to the simple life of Walden Island.

There was Ruth Kirk, the nature writer, who dedicated her seminal work, *The Olympic Rainforest*, to Minnie.

There was her husband, Oscar, who understood Minnie, taught her everything she knew (her admission), and without whom Minnie's Grand Adventure would not have been possible.

And, of course, there were Minnie's children and grandchildren, who owe her so much.

So many rode the high places with Minnie and were refreshed by those memories the rest of their lives. For years they came to Minnie's cabin on the Hoh to pay homage, relive a happy time or play a game of cards or a game of chess.

ACKNOWLEDGEMENTS

Special thanks to the following:

- Oscar Peterson Jr. for his stories.

- Sandy Floe and George Brown for their written contributions to the project.

- Cougar Fields for his stories and pictures.

- Olympic National Park, Olympic National Forest and Clallam County Historical Society for making their resources available to the authors.

- Stan Burrowes for invaluable historical knowledge he shared so generously.

- Charlotte Peterson for providing inspiration and artistic expertise.

- John Carter for the genealogical information he compiled.

- Will Muller for the timely, in-depth interview he elicited from Minnie.

- Sandy Patton, who freely shared her memories of twenty years as Minnie's confidant.

- Monica Henry for her editing recommendations.

- Trevor Henry for his management of all technical aspects of the project from photo restoration to publication lay-out.

FORWARD

November 16, 1979 was a cold, gray day in the Hoh River Valley. Glynda Peterson and her sister-in-law, Charlotte Peterson, sat across the table from Minnie Peterson in her cozy Hoh River cabin. They listened as Minnie plotted high country adventure for the 1980 season, trips that would never happen. At 82, the rigors of the back country had caught up with Minnie. Glynda and Charlotte were listening also for something else, and just after 11:00 a.m., they heard it. A distant hum grew to the clatter of prop wash that rattled the dining room windows. An accompanying whine decreased as the helicopter's engine power was cut. A minute later Dick Kimball "Whisper" stepped into the room bundled in heavy clothing and recommending the same for his passengers. Soon they were all packed into the 4-seater. After strapping Minnie into the forward passenger seat, Whisper fired up the jet engine.

For the next hour, from that plexiglass bubble, they saw it all again. Whisper flew over Bogachiel Peak and the three river valleys that converge there. Minnie pointed out the High Divide Trail as it crossed the meadows west of Cat Peak and Mt. Carrie. In the distance, a stout lone bear moved lazily toward the timberline below the trail. North of the High Divide, Minnie pointed out her old friends: Deer and Heart Lakes, Minnie Peterson Ridge (where her cabin was built), Seven Lakes Basin, Cat Creek Basin and Sol Duc Park. Nestled deep in the valley below lay the Sol Duc Resort.

At 5000 feet, the November cold seeped through the glass and metal wall of the aircraft. It was in the twenties outside and not much warmer inside, though no one spoke of the cold so dazzling was the scenery, white with the season's first dusting of snow. Across the Divide and over the Hoh again, Mt. Olympus and its hanging glaciers loomed large to the south. At over 100 miles per hour and less than a mile away the Mount Olympus massif flew by: the Hoh, Ice River, and Blue Glaciers, the Snow Dome, Panic Peak and White Glacier all in their turn.

Whisper flew past Mt. Tom and pulled up next to Hoh Peak, then dropped into the "mystical"* and remote headwaters of the South Fork of the Hoh River. This region is without roads or trails and is fiercely guarded to the east and south by the rock sentinels of the Valhallas.** Thor, Hugin, Woden, Munin, Frigga and the gravity defying Loki Spire protect the privacy of the tumbling cascade of Valkyrie Creek as well as the vertical ice of the Geri-Freki Glacier and the hidden valley below it. To the north, the south wall of Mt. Olympus dominated the landscape.

Whisper made a final turn west and flew over multiple bands of elk visible through the old growth, then pointed the aircraft down valley toward the light green opening that was Minnie's ranch.

In less than an hour that day in November, Charlotte, Glynda and Minnie saw it all again: the stage, the set and the scenery for a play that ran for fifty seasons.

---

*   Chris Morganroth's word for the South Fork.
**   In 1978 the last first ascents were done here at the cost of one climber's life.

Minnie - 1910

Sister Helma - 1908

Minnie - 1908

Hoko Homestead - 1910

Nels Nelson - 1910

Brother Bill Nelson - 1917

Nelson Women - 1911
Minnie, Sophia, Ada, Helma

Winifred and Eli Peterson on their wedding day - 1882

Peterson Homestead on the Forks Prairie - 1899

Oscar Peterson - 1903

Peterson Family - 1899
Oscar, Eli, Myrtle, Morton, Elma, Winifred

Clallam Bay - 1910

CHAPTER ONE

BEYOND THE HOKO

Papa Nels Nelson had kept his promise. A new house was waiting for them in Clallam Bay with new store bought furnishings. There were streets with shops and neighbors and cars. A steam ship came every week from Seattle. For Minnie it was all very nice in Clallam Bay but in town the bear, elk, deer and cougar were gone and the big trees had already been cut, all the way down to the salt water. Minnie was sixteen, however, and there were those dances in Forks which meant overnights with friends. There were also those Peterson boys. Morton was the life of every party in Forks but it was Oscar who made her laugh and entertained her with stories of lost gold and stage coach robberies. Most of all she liked to hear about the wild places in the high Olympics. Oscar had been to the upper most reaches of the Sol Duc Valley, to a basin filled with lakes and to another adjacent basin with a single lake shaped like a heart. Between the lakes

and to the ridge tops were thousands of acres of wild flowers. A mile below the ridge, the Hoh wound its way west down a wide valley. Across the valley the many summits of Mount Olympus rose out of permanent snows. Deer, elk, marmots, wolves and of course, mountain lions, roamed the landscape.

Mama Sophia and Papa Nels were a little more down to earth. The forest was a fine place for a picnic but it was 1914 and they were town people now. Minnie needed to complete her education. A little more civilizing would not hurt either. So it was that in the fall of 1914 Minnie was sent to boarding high school at State College of Washington. She lived in Stevens Hall, enjoyed women's field hockey, and loved spending time with her good friend, Myrtle Westlund. The bare, rolling Palouse hills, however, were no substitute for the Olympics and none of the boys held a candle to Oscar. Furthermore, there were as many rules as at West Point and a stern battle axe house mother to enforce them. At semester break Minnie returned home to Clallam Bay and began cooking for her father's road construction crew.

On June 4, 1915 Minnie married Oscar Peterson and they moved in across the road from the three-story Peterson family farm house.* Oscar helped with the family farm, worked as the town's blacksmith and continued to guide in the summer.

Minnie and Myrtle (Westlund) Walkling - 1914

---

* Nels would not give Minnie and Oscar permission to marry until Oscar had built a house.

State College of Washington woman's field hockey team
Minnie front row, third from right - 1914

Eli Peterson farm - 1915
Note: Minnie and Oscar's house far left

Eli Peterson farmhouse - 1916

June 4, 1915
Wedding Day - Minnie and Oscar

For those concerned about Minnie's free spirit, seeing her settle into a domestic routine was a relief. Her mother-in-law, Winifred, was the descendent of a long-standing and very civilized Ford family from the East. In addition, Minnie's house was surrounded by over 300 acres of Peterson family farm that represented considerable wealth. She soon realized that this new environment represented routine, predictability, dusting and cleaning, long dresses and fancy shoes that would not take her where she wanted to go. Minnie was soon plotting her escape to the high, wild places she had heard so much about. For the trek she recruited her sister-in-law, Myrtle Peterson, to keep the appearance of propriety, and half dozen local mountain men.

Seventy years later, Minnie's eyes lit up as she recalled their fun, far away from the clucking hens of Forks. It was a better place than Oscar had described and exceeded all her expectations. The mountain lakes, streams, lush alpine meadows, stunning views and good friends made the trip more wonderful than Minnie could have imagined. From their camp on the High Divide to the north lay Vancouver Island, to the west, the Hoh River Valley and the Pacific, and to the east, the peaks of the Bailey Range. But it was the view to the south that was the most extraordinary, always drawing the eye back from other distractions. In the immediate foreground were alpine meadows full of vibrant color and across the valley, Mt. Olympus, finely cut ice set in stone. Crown jewel of all the Olympics.

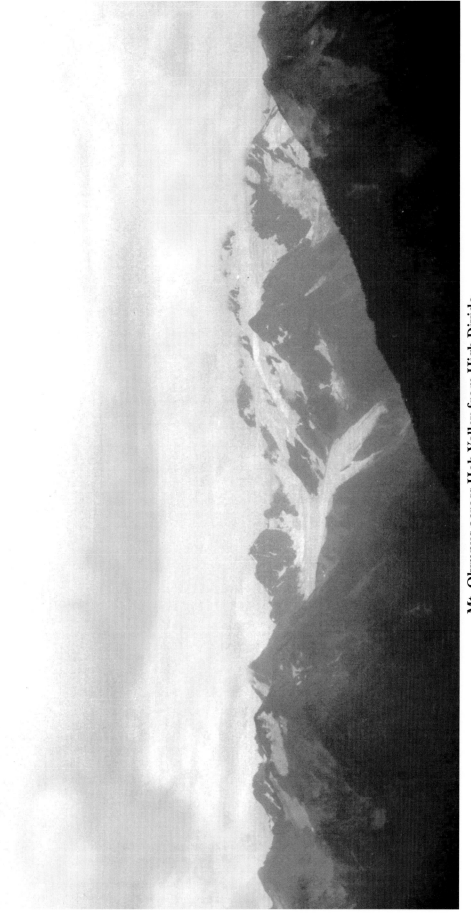

Mt. Olympus across Hoh Valley from High Divide

Blue Glacier on Mt. Olympus

High Divide - North Slope
Mt. Carrie in background

Minnie and hiking recruits - 1915

In its shadow the adventurers descended into the Hoh Valley. The map showed a zigzag trail but it was more like a ski hill with steep loose shale slopes instead of snow. Rolling their packs ahead of themselves, the hikers moved down the shale slope until it gave way to forest. The view from the ridge top had only hinted at the wonders in this valley. This was a forest unlike any Minnie had ever seen. Recently, the trail had been cut through a tangle of vines and huge windfall. No one dare wander off the path because at five yards the trail disappeared and at ten, it ceased to exist. Furthermore, that inviting purchase in this jungle could easily be devil's club disguised by a little rainforest moss. Unlike nettle, the wound of the devil's club ached with a seemingly eternal pain.* Saint and sinner agree that devil's clubs would make an appropriate landscaping plant for the gates of Hell.

The rest of the forest, however, was Minnie's vision of Heaven. The trail wound through spruce, hemlock and cedar trees, many more than two-hundred feet tall and twelve feet in diameter. Grazing on red and blue huckleberries, blackberries, and blackcaps proved to be the best part of the trek down the river valley. After a night in the meadow where Olympus Guard Station was built later in 1918 (now identified as Lewis Meadow), the intrepid hikers proceeded to the John Huelsdonk (Iron Man) homestead where they were greeted by John and Dora and two of their daughters, Elizabeth and Marie.

Not long after Minnie arrived home, Oscar came to grips with the fact that the Minnie who went into the backcountry was not the same Minnie who returned from the Olympic Wilderness that summer of 1915. Minnie had met and fallen in love with the second great love of her life-the wild places of the high Olympics. From that time forward, Minnie's loyalty and affection were divided.

Hikers greeted by the Huelsdonk family - 1915
Dora, Myrtle Peterson, Marie, Minnie P., Elizabeth, John, unknown

---

*   Pain often lasts ten days to two weeks.

Cottage Hotel in Forks - 1915
Fannie Taylor Photo

8

Cottage Hotel in Forks - 1916
C.J. Albrecht Photo

Preparing for the California motorcycle trip - 1915

Because of Oscar's summer commitments on the Peterson farm, Oscar and Minnie's wedding trip was planned for the fall after the oat harvest and timed so they could take in the Panama Pacific International Expedition in San Francisco. Since pants would have landed her in jail in many towns along the way, Minnie bought a divided skirt and rode tandem on Oscar's new 1914 Indian motorcycle.

They made 130 miles the first day out of Forks spending the night of September 20th in Quilcene. Post cards from this stop reflect a positive mood although much of the route traveled was little more than rough trail. Similar road conditions continued throughout the trip. Flat tires were a daily occurrence. The amazing expo in San Francisco, however, was a wonderland for the couple and the pains of the trip were soon forgotten. In mid-October Minnie and Oscar returned to Puget Sound on a steam ship. No flats on the trip north, but lots of bed bugs.

Arch of the Rising Sun - Court of the Universe at the Panama Pacific International Exposition - 1915

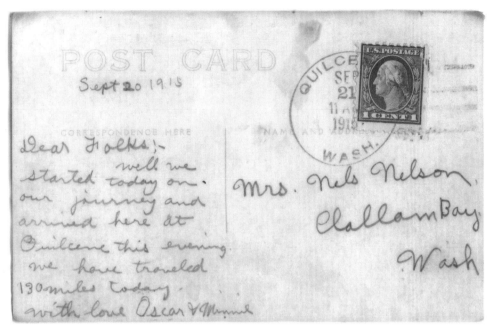

POST CARD

Sept 20 1915

CORRESPONDENCE HERE

Dear Folks:-
well we
started today on
our journey and
arrived here at
Quilcene this evening
we have traveled
130 miles today.
with love Oscar & Minnie

Mrs. Nels Nelson,
Clallam Bay,
Wash

Postcard from Quilcene

NO 1055 AT QUILCENE.

First stop on honeymoon trip - September 20, 1915

Minnie and Oscar's home in Forks

Tragedy struck the Peterson family in September of 1916 when Eli, the patriarch of the family, was killed in a car accident. The family farm was partitioned and Oscar and Minnie were given a "forty" on the southeast corner of Forks Prairie. They moved their starter house to this property, enlarged it and eventually built a barn, blacksmith's shop, and other outbuildings. Subsequently the couple set about the tasks of raising children, sheep and cattle. Oscar continued his blacksmith work for the locals and contract packing for the US Forest Service, road contractors, and surveyors. Oscar's work often led him on adventures that afterwards he would describe to Minnie. Although a very practical man in many ways, Oscar enjoyed dreaming of adventure, of discovering buried treasure, of finding gold or oil.

Oscar trucking grain. - 1915
Note: Congregational steeple in the background.

Oscar's brother, Morton, with Forks Prairie produce - 1915

Eli and sons in hay harvest - 1915

New Year's Costume Party - 1918

Back row: Mabel Parker, Sherman Parker, Charlotte Klahn, Myrtle Peterson, Katheryn Shearer, Minnie Peterson, Oscar Peterson, Skinner, Frank Gaydeski, Butch Krogh, Bill Iverson

Middle row: Cliff Wilson, Violet Kidd, Mrs. Krogh, Mr. Kidd, Martin Rahm, School Teacher, Mrs. Floyd Ross, Uncle Sam, Teeley Taylor, Steve Gaydeski, Mary Wilson, Earl Wilson

Front: School Teacher, M. Smith, Miss Hess (Hawk), Unknown, Mrs. Cliff Wilson

15

Minnie at home with Ivan and Vivian - 1920

Four little lambs - 1920

"Oompa Loompas"

Ivan with hog - 1920

C.J. Albrecht arrives in Forks - Fall 1916
C.J. Albrecht photo

While Minnie assumed the responsibilities of family and farm, Oscar accepted occasional work packing for Clarence Albrecht who had first come to the Olympics in 1914 in search of specimens for the huge dioramas at the Chicago Field Museum. In the fall of 1916 Clarence returned, determined to hunt the "Big One." He wanted a trophy elk as well as other large mammals for the "mother of all dioramas." After hiring LeRoy Smith and Oscar to help, ten pack horses were assembled. Base camp was established two days ride from Forks at Fred Fisher's Hoh River Ranch, close to what is now the Olympic Park boundary.

On the river bar (near the present Hoh Ranger Station), Clarence found the big bull elk he was looking for. Shortly thereafter, the joy of a successful hunt was somewhat tempered for Clarence and Oscar and considerably diminished for LeRoy. Leroy's pack horse, Kitty, taking great exception to being loaded with bloody hide and horn, broke its one inch tie down rope, bucked off its pack, swam the Hoh River, and was last seen making tracks over a gravel bar on the river's south bank.

Time and events in the back country seal friendships that last decades. The fifty year plus relationship between the Petersons and Albrechts confirmed this principle. Minnie's son, Oscar Clarence, and daughter, Carma, were namesakes of the Albrechts.

Carma at Sol Duc - 1940's

18

Albrecht expedition base camp - 1916
C.J. Albrecht photo

Oscar on Hoh River trail to base camp - 1916
C.J. Albrecht photo

Olympic Rainforest diarama - Chicago Field Museum - 1918
C.J. Albrecht photo

Another Oscar escapade was shared with Minnie's only brother, Bill. Upon returning from the Western Front of WWI in 1919, Brother Bill was elected Sheriff of Clallam County. Soon after, he showed up in Forks looking for a posse. (There had been a murder at Discovery Bay and the perpetrators had been seen traveling west.) Bill checked the hangouts in town but found no volunteers. By the time he located Oscar, Bill's view of Forks civic pride had dimmed. Oscar, however, always ready for a little excitement, wanted to "get the show on the road." He kissed Minnie goodbye, grabbed his 30-30 and saddled his horse. In less time than it takes to tell it, the sheriff and his posse of one were riding hard for the killers' hideout on the Bogachiel River.

Arriving early, Billy waited for smoke to come from the chimney, guessing that the duo would have started a fire to cook breakfast. With his gun still holstered, Billy kicked the door in and ordered the outlaws to get their hands in the air. The fugitives hesitated, noticing that Bill had no gun in hand. The hesitation was momentary, however. At the same instant one of the killer's gun hand twitched, all heard the sound of Oscar thumbing back the hammer of his 30-30. To speed the trip back to Forks Billy did not cuff the outlaws; instead, he emphasized to them the advantages to Jefferson County taxpayers if the coroner, rather than the judge, was the first to see them in Port Townsend.*

Sheriff Bill Nelson proudly displays bootlegger's still seized in a raid - 1923

---

* They were sentenced to life at Walla Walla State Penitentiary. Sheriff William Nelson, Minnie's only brother, died from injuries sustained in the line of duty in 1924.

To Minnie -
Please enjoy
Harriet Fish

Dedicated To Clallam County's
Twenty-first Sheriff
Billy Nelson

Kellogg

- Served Clallam County as Sheriff: 1920 - 1924
- Was youngest Sheriff in the county's history
- First white boy born on upper Hoko River
- World War I — Army Corps of Engineers
- Captured Sequim bank robbers in March 1922
- Captured murderers of Discovery Bay logger at Hoh River in 1922
- Destroyed large scale stills during prohibition
- Father: Nels Nelson, Mother: Helma Nelson
- Died at 28, during second term as Sheriff — death caused from duty related injury

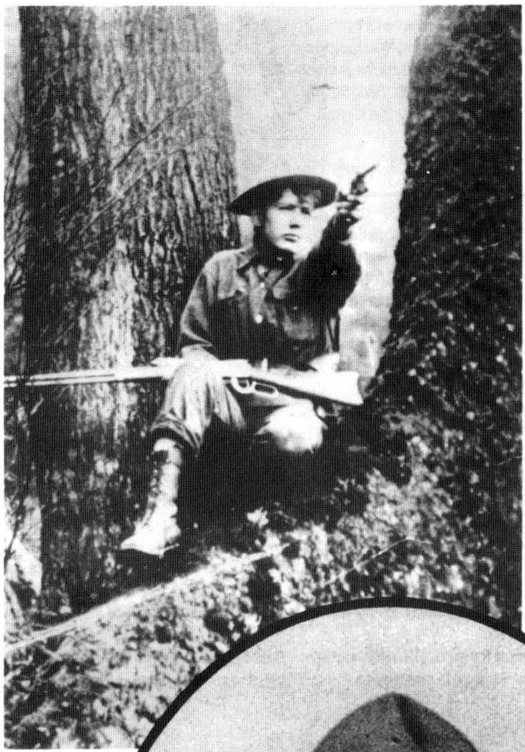

True Detective Mysteries · Feb. 1933

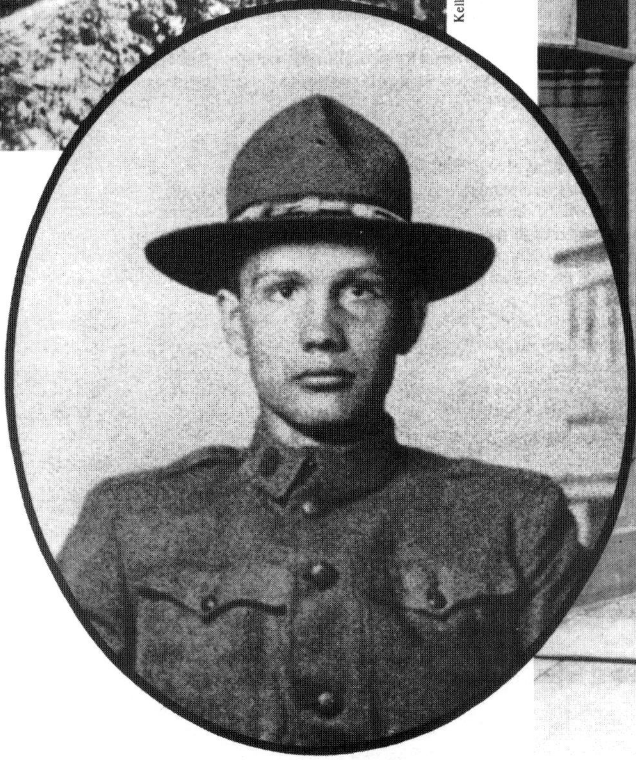

Billy as Sheriff during the early 1920's

Kellogg

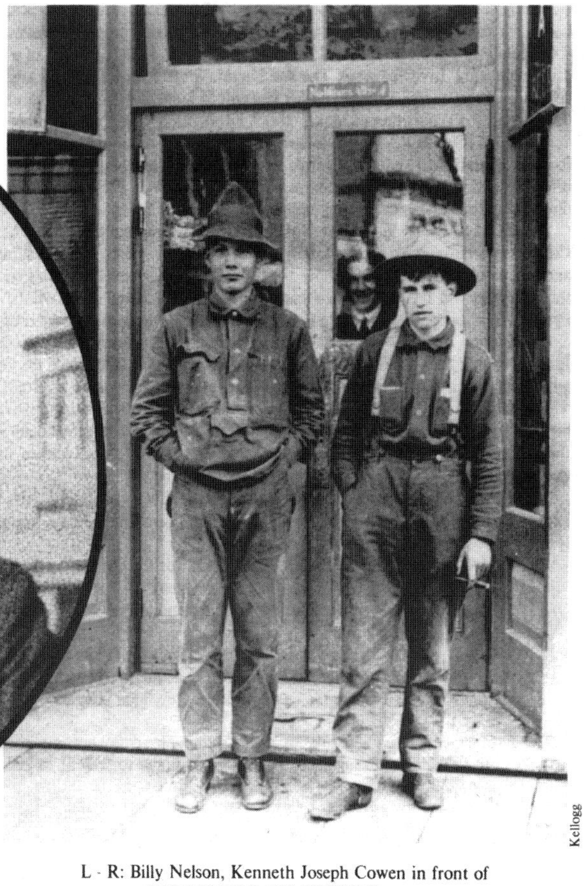

L - R: Billy Nelson, Kenneth Joseph Cowen in front of "NO MINORS ALLOWED" Tavern.

Courtesy of Clallam County Sheriff's Department

CHAPTER TWO

THE EARLY TUMULTUOUS, TRIUMPHANT TWENTIES.

On January 29, 1921, 3:22 p.m., at North Head on Grays Harbor, the anemometer quit after recording 126 mph winds. Minutes later, the Lone Tree Bureau, also at Grays Harbor, recorded 140 mph winds for three minutes and then exploded. At 6:30 p.m. the same day in Forks, Minnie was at home with her young children, Vivian and Ivan. Dusk was turning to darkness when there arose from the southwest a thunderous, cataclysmic, apocalyptic, earth shattering sustained explosion. It was the sound of hundreds of square miles of old growth timber being broken and uprooted and thrown through the air. It was also the sound of houses and barns being crushed. And Oscar was out in it.

Downed timber - 1921 Blow

Peterson barn and silo - 1921 Blow

Peterson windmill after 1921 Blow

Oscar and Tom Newton had set out on foot that afternoon for Shuwah Prairie, three miles north of Forks. According to Chris Morganroth, when the storm hit, trees, five to seven feet through, were falling all around them. They jumped from side to side to avoid being hit. Quickly realizing that this strategy would surely get them killed, Oscar and Tom ran, jumped, and climbed to reach the open prairie. They arrived just as a huge flying tree top came hurtling down impaling the earth so close to Tom that he could not stop before colliding with it. Later while surveying the destruction, the top was found to be sunk four feet into the earth. Tom was bruised and dazed but otherwise okay and Oscar survived unscathed. By Chris Morganroth's count, several houses as well as eighteen barns in the area collapsed. Roads and trails were blocked in every direction out of Forks and cars enroute to Port Angeles were either trapped or crushed. Eight billion board feet of timber lay shattered on the ground. Oscar and Minnie lost four head of cattle, a serious blow to the young family but a lucky break compared to what others suffered. Minnie's mother-in-law tallied her losses:

- 1 Dairy barn
- 1 Silo
- 36 Cows and yearlings
- 1 Holstein bull
- 1 Auto
- 1 Truck
- 2 Grindstones
- 4 Sets of harnesses
- 400 Sacks of oats
- 1 Windmill and tower
- Many small items

Total loss $8,000=Today's dollars $250,000

Puncheon trail destruction - 1921 Blow

Minnie and Oscar dodged some well aimed bullets in the twenties and did not always come away unscathed. The same was true of their friends. Myrtle Westlund Walkling, Minnie's bosom buddy and friend from their boarding school days in Pullman, had continued to visit and write. Her letters express both a longing for country life as well as quite progressive political leanings. Although as a student she is absorbed by campus social life, (1916 letter in appendix) by 1919 her letters exhibit what appears to be genuine concern for unemployed soldiers just home from Europe after WWI. "As far as I'm concerned I'd rather see them go ahead and get the boy a job rather than giving them dances, etc." (1919 letter in appendix)

In addition to being socially conscious, Myrtle had an adventurous spirit that rivaled Minnie's. But while Minnie kept her feet planted firmly on the ground or in stirrups, Myrtle took to the air with near fatal results. The circumstances surrounding Myrtle and Ben's Sept. 28, 1922 crash are not known but the pictures of the aftermath speak for themselves.

In Myrtle's words the couple's escape was—miraculous. We now know this was not just a narrow escape for Ben and Myrtle but was a close call for future generations in Clallam County who would benefit from the philanthropy of this generous couple.*

Down on the farm - 1921
Clockwise: Ivan, Vivian, Minnie and Myrtle

"Remains of the flight of Myrtle and Ben" - **Myrtle Walkling**
Photo taken after victims were transported to hospital.

---

* The Ben and Myrtle Walkling Trust continues to this day to fund scholarships for local students as well as grants for important community projects.

Times were good for Myrtle and Ben in the roaring twenties. From 1925 to 1942 the couple owned and managed Walkling Motor Company in Port Angeles.

Myrtle's notation back of photo:
"This will give you a vague idea of the miraculous escape we made."
September 28, 1922

Myrtle Peterson greets pilots as they come in from fire patrol - 1921.
The Peterson farm served as headquarters for fire suppression and control efforts.

Biological Survey Expedition - 1921

Death and destruction did not entirely define the twenties. There were significant discoveries to be made and Oscar and Minnie had a part to play. In the early twentieth century the flora and fauna of the inner Olympic Peninsula remained a mystery. Curiosity in this matter within the Department of Agriculture finally came to a head in 1920 and funds were allocated for a study. Walter P. Taylor and his associate, George Cantwell, from the US Biological Survey (USDA) recruited Harold St. John, a professor of Botany with a spanking new PhD. from Harvard, and William T. Shaw, a noted Zoologist, (both from the State College of Washington) for a ten week Olympic Expedition. Oscar was contracted as their guide and packer at $40 per horse per month.

Camp photos - 1921 expedition

On the way to the Elwha - Olympic Hot Springs
1921 Biological Survey

Oscar surveys the world below.
1921 Biological Survey Expedition

Near Bogachiel Peak

UNITED STATES DEPARTMENT OF AGRICULTURE
BUREAU OF BIOLOGICAL SURVEY

IN REPLY REFER TO

Sol Duc, Wash.
Sept. 9, 1921

To Whom It may Concern:

This is to certify that Oscar Peterson of Forks, Wash. has been in the employ of the Biological Survey Party continuously as packer and guide from July 1, 1921 to date, and we take pleasure in presenting him with this unsolicited testimonial signifying our appreciation of his uniformly courteous and efficient services. He has at all times labored to promote the work in accordance with our wishes, and has remained cordially helpful through the stress and strain of all sorts of camp conditions, favorable and unfavorable.

Walter P. Taylor, U.S. Biological Survey
Harold St John, Asst. Prof. of Botany.
Geo. G. Cantwell, U.S. Biological Survey
W.T. Shaw, Zoologist, State College of Washington

"Letting the rest of the world roll by."
caption on original photograph
1921 Biological Survey photo

"Who's got the laugh on us, eh Oscar?"
caption on original photograph
1921 Biological Survey photo

In 1924 Oscar enhanced his guiding resume further by participating in the attempt mounted to rescue Joe Jeffers from the slopes of Mt. Olympus. In the first quarter of the twentieth century Jeffers became quite well-known in the Northwest for photography. He and his family recorded the history of the Olympia area from 1905-1973 on negatives. Jeffers was also legendary for his daring. In his son Joe Jr.'s words, "He provoked danger with impunity." As an example he sighted his father's fondness for racing trains to crossings.

This man with nine lives used his ninth on the five thousand foot southern wall of Mt. Olympus while attempting with his son, Vibert, a descent into the South Fork of the Hoh River via Hubert Glacier. In the midst of a pendulum move on a short rope, Jeffers fell into a cavernous crevasse between rock and ice. In an amazing feat of mountaineering, Vibert soloed a chimney in the wall above and regained the Mt. Olympus Plateau at seven thousand feet, then returned to the terminus of the Blue Glacier where a trail crew was working. The following day, August 24, Charlie Lewis and another USFS employee accompanied Vibert back to the scene of the accident. It was obvious to Charlie that nothing could be done from this approach.

Joe was well thought of and thus quite connected in Olympia, so by the 28th of August a rescue/body-recovery team had assembled in Forks. Led by Swiss mountaineer Heinie Fuhrer from Mt. Rainier National Park, the group included another Swiss as well as Neil McKay, Frank Weir, local folks, and twelve year old Virgil Brandeberry. By some accounts there were ten in the party, by others, twenty.* Fuhrer contracted Oscar as guide and packer.

Base camp for Jeffers rescue looking east. Camp located north of the Boulder Field. South Fork of the Hoh runs south of the Boulder Field.

Today the South Fork Hoh Valley is as mysterious as it is remote. In 1924 it was a hard two day ride to the river from Forks and an exhausting day of bushwhacking through two canyons before the rescuers and pack train arrived at the Boulder Field** where base camp was established. The following morning Virgil*** was left with the horses and a pistol while the rest of the group pushed ahead into a world of glacial basins, snow, ice, and rock. They made visual contact with a group that Chris Morganroth had sent up Olympus by the standard route and spent the next two days**** attempting an approach to the bergschrund. Steep ice and crevasses in the Hubert and crumbling perpendicular rock combined to frustrate the mountaineers and on September 3rd they retreated, arriving back in Forks on September 5th. The reward for Jeffer's body went uncollected. At the time of his death it was reported by friends that Joe Jeffers had often related the hope that in the end, Mt. Olympus would be his sepulcher. His wish was granted and Joe's name immortalized by the naming of Jeffers Glacier.

*   The literature is conflicted on the details of this accident and subsequent rescue attempt.
**   South Fork Boulder Field-a geologic formation of house-sized boulders
*** Virgil claimed 60 years later to have found two wolf dens in his exploration of the area. (as told to Stan Peterson)
**** Some accounts say two weeks but that is not consistent with Oscar's day book entries.

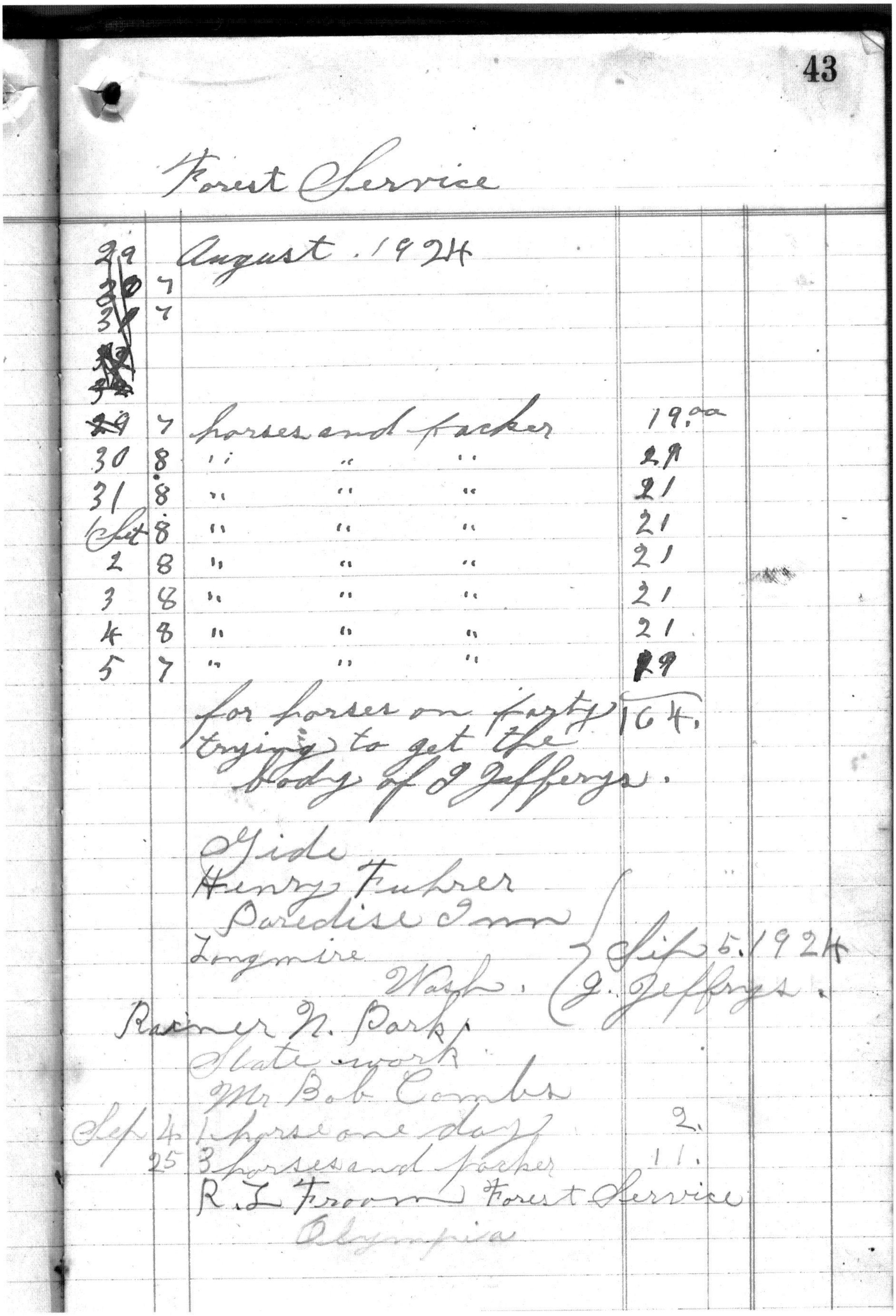

Forest Service

August . 1924

29			
30	7		
31	7		
29	7	horses and packer	19.00
30	8	" " "	21
31	8	" " "	21
Sept	8	" " "	21
2	8	" " "	21
3	8	" " "	21
4	8	" " "	21
5	7	" " "	19

for horses on packf | 164.
trying to get the
body of J Jeffers.

Gide
Henry Fuhrer
Paradise Inn
Longmire
Wash.
Rainer N. Park.
State work
Mr Bob Comber
Sep 4 1 horse one day | 2.
25 3 horses and packer | 11.
R L Froom Forest Service
Olympia

} Sep 5. 1924
J. Jeffers.

Oscar Peterson's daybook entries for Jeffers rescue

CHAPTER THREE

A PERSONAL DISTANCE RECORD, BOSCO, AND THE BIRTH OF A LIFE-LONG VOCATION.

The world was changing fast in the early twenties and civilization was rapidly approaching the West End. Trails were being replaced by roads; horses and wagons, by cars and trucks. However, in 1924 and 1925 Oscar made very good money, as is documented by his daybook. He charged four dollars a day for himself and $1.50 per day per pack horse averaging nearly fourteen dollars a day for the 177 days his string was on the trail in 1925. Most of the packing was contract work for the State Highway Department. Ira C. Otis was the man in charge. Oscar moved material, equipment and food to various surveying, engineering, and construction camps along the proposed Highway 101 route, south of Forks. As road construction progressed, Oscar worked himself out of a job as a traditional freighter and packer.

Oscar, packing for State Highway Department, heads to Ruby Beach through Forks.

There were, however, other opportunities. Since the interior of the Peninsula remained roadless, a good pack horse was still in demand. Glines Canyon Dam on the Elwha was in the early stages of development. The road to the dam site from Highway 101 had not been built but preliminary work had begun on both the dam and its reservoir. Workers needed camp supplies and equipment for the project. Northwest Power Company awarded the packing contract to Oscar and established a storehouse near the Old Covered Bridge (about one mile up river from the current Highway 101 bridge). Oscar moved some supplies from the storehouse to a camp near the dam site, while other supplies went to camps located farther south on the future lake bed.

Oscar moves camp behind Glines Canyon Dam - 1926

37

The work was brutal but steady. In one letter Oscar writes that it is midnight and he had been on the trail until 10 p.m. packing pumps and equipment to a crew at the south end of the lake bed where a slash fire was burning out of control. In the same letter dated June 22, 1926, he promises Minnie fresh Elwha Valley venison on his next trip to Forks.

Elwha, Wash.
June 22, 1926

Dear Minnie,

This is Tuesday night I sure been a real busy boy today. They let the fire get away from them up at Wright camp this afternoon so I had to make three trips up there since three o'clock. Gas, hose and pumps I got back Sunday when the meeting was all most through. We are going to try to get in to the mine about the first of August. I will tell you the next time I come home that will maybe be before Sunday I hope, maybe not. I will bring some meat in. I seen two nice buck deer last night right here at camp. If I had a rope and a horse I think I could have roped him. He would likely cut up more than that calf we caught on the Bogachiel road last year. I got the Forest Service job, so Joe Stanley told me today.

I am sending a horse up to Humes ranch tomorrow to pack out a live cougar. Well Minnie dear I've told you all the news that has happened since Sunday so will close old Dear as I sure am tired tonight I mean night it is after twelve as I did not yet get back until after ten. Bye Bye

Lovingly yours,

Oscar Peterson

According to Minnie, Ranger Chris Morganroth had concerns about Oscar's hunting habits and often scrutinized Oscar as he unloaded his pack horses. Chris was never able to confirm his suspicions. Late in August Oscar packed a special treat to the Elwha camp. The big, smoked, bone-in ham had the loggers drooling as they helped unpack. It was then hung very high, away from varmints. The cook assured the crew they would be eating it the following evening. Dreams that night were filled with ham dinner and all the fixings. It was not to be. The next day, after the cook put a razor's edge on his best carving knife, he went outside to recover the ham. He quickly realized something was dreadfully wrong. What was left of the ham was blowing lightly in the breeze while yellow jackets swarmed around picking the last flesh off a gleaming white bone.

On the home front Minnie had given birth to the youngest of the Peterson children. Carma was born on May 26, 1926 and three months later, after receiving word that Oscar needed an additional pack horse, Minnie completed a personal distance record that stood the rest of her life. She rode 58 miles from Forks to Oscar's Elwha camp in twenty hours.*

---

*   Twenty miles is a good day on horse back.

Elwha camp on lake bed

Note: Smoke from slash burns left - center of picture. - 1926

View of crane and gondola from canyon floor - 1926

It is difficult to reconcile what Minnie accomplished in her life with her motto "never let work get in the way of pleasure" unless one understands the sheer joy she got out of living and the degree to which she blurred the lines between work and fun. Oscar was of a similar mind. The big crane that swung out over the 200 foot Glines Canyon inspired his imagination. He acquired the necessary permission, probably expedited with a couple quarts of bootleg whiskey, and in that summer of 1926, Oscar and Minnie took the ride of their lives two hundred feet above the raging Elwha River.*

---

*   The assumption is made that this ride took place some time before the tragic construction accident that killed six and maimed several more workers. (See Olympic National Park archives Neil Pendley interview by Jacilee Wray)

Late stage dam construction

Glines Canyon Dam is completed - 1927

    Minnie also enjoyed the adrenaline rush of a good game (cards, dice, chess, checkers) and, of course, a wager just to keep things interesting. The fact of the matter was that Minnie would bet on anything if she liked the odds. The following, however, is not so much a tribute to Minnie's gambling prowess, but a tribute to her ability to keep a poker face.

Oscar always the showman - Sol Duc cabin 1930

Of all the horses in Oscar's string, one caught Minnie's eye. Oscar called the gelding Bosco. Oscar had trained him to go anywhere in the mountains. He had also been taught to walk up the steps on the porch of the cabin at Sol Duc, and on occasion Oscar even allowed him inside the cabin. Oscar rode Bosco and Bay Bill, another horse, at the same time, standing one foot on each horse. This act offered great entertainment for Sol Duc tourists. Bosco was strong, smart and fast and Minnie wanted, in the worst way, to call him her own.

Oscar's antics - Sol Duc - late twenties

Early in 1927 Oscar made his annual trip to Seattle for supplies. While in Seattle he shopped at Pike Street Farmer's Market where he picked up a big bag of pineapples. He knew this would please Minnie. On his return Oscar figured he would have a little fun with Minnie and so as soon as he arrived home he invited her to guess what was in the bag. She replied that she was willing to wager that she did know what was in the bag. Oscar was certain enough himself to put his Bosco on the table against anything Minnie was willing to bet. Now Oscar was a heavy smoker (unfiltered Camels). Between the smoke and the chew, his sense of smell was pretty much gone and so he failed to realize that not only the front room, but the entire house, was filled with the sweet aroma of ripe pineapple. The next day Minnie's saddle was on Bosco.

In the spring of 1927 the need to diversify his packing business became apparent to Oscar. His work for the Forest Service was not going to keep the horses busy. As the roads improved and the need for pack horses diminished, the country was beginning to enjoy the mobility of the auto.

Sol Duc, a place enjoyed exclusively by the rich in the 1910's, was accessible to everyone in the twenties and eventually developed a loyal clientele from Puget Sound and Grays Harbor. In his Sol Duc literature, C.F. Martin recommended stays of one to two weeks or more to get the full benefit of the springs. The ads announced daily recreation opportunities including fishing, hiking, swimming, tennis, baseball and dancing. An experienced masseur was also on staff. C.F. only needed a string of saddle horses to complete the package. Oscar made arrangements to locate his headquarters at a farm a mile below the Sol Duc. Soon after, he moved his horses from Forks to the farm and the first steps toward developing an outfitting business commenced.

Second Sol Duc Hotel, also destroyed by fire.

Covered end of pool at Sol Duc - 1927

Sol Duc visitors out for a ride - late twenties

Day ride to Bogachiel from Sol Duc - late twenties

Oscar guides Mt. Olympus climb - Summer 1927
W. Bailey photo

Hmmm. It looks pretty deep!
W. Bailey photo

W. Bailey on Blue Glacier

48

Summit of West Peak on Mt. Olympus - 1927
Bailey party.
W. Bailey photo

The Bailey party
Mt. Olympus climb - 1927
W. Bailey photo

49

For rugged mountain beauty, the Olympics rank second to none. Nature was in a most lavish mood when she bestowed all the wealth of scenic beauty which is to be seen here. Today its rugged beauty remains as in ages gone by, for the hand of man has not come to mar this marvelous work of nature.

Forest service trails wind their way through the virgin stands of timber and over mountain tops. These trails are always kept open and are easily followed. From Sol Duc, over 300 miles of open trail wend their way.

From Sol Duc two trails originate. One of them, the Bogachiel Park Trail, heads west over mountain and through a dense stand of virgin forest. Finally after a short hike you come to Mink Lake, a beautiful lake laying between the mountains and fed by innumerable springs flowing into it from under its grassy banks. Further out the trail crosses mountain meadows and then switchbacks sharply up a mountain, leaving the lake far below. More meadow and another climb, you find yourself on top of the Little Divide. Crossing the divide the most wonderful of all sights in the Olympics greets the eye. Mt. Olympus, and its eternally snow-capped peaks, glisten in the sun with the blue sky for its background. Here also the mountains are ablaze with the color of wild flowers, thousands of them covering the mountain slopes. Further along the trail a look down into Blackwood Lake is to be had. Resembling a sapphire in an emerald setting the lake lies a thousand feet below. This is about as far as one will wish to travel over this trail and back again in one day, so further description of it is of no necessity.

The second trail which leaves the camp is known as the Canyon Creek-Hoh Trail. This trail takes you through virgin forest, following the Soleduck River back to Soleduck Falls, a hike that anyone can make. Here the trail crosses the canyon at the falls and then follows its way up Canyon Creek, passing many small waterfalls on the way. Finally you arrive at Deer Lake, another mountain jewel. Crossing the high Soleduck Divide, you come to the Seven Lakes region, a region awe-inspiring in its rugged beauty. From here such a panoramic view of mountain peaks are to be seen that will never be forgotten. On clear days it is possible to see the blue expanse of the Pacific Ocean far off to the west. Now the trail passes along the west face of Bogachiel Peak, across a connecting ridge to another peak and after going around to the far side and gazing down into Hoh Lake, the most beautiful of all lakes in the Olympics, you are ready for the return journey back to camp. From this point Mt. Olympus is but six miles distant on an air line. A most wonderful view is to be had of the north face of it. A trip this far out on the trail is usually made by horseback, and it uses up an entire day. Many thrills are to be had along the way and the thousands of flowers which line the trail and mountain slopes are beautiful, beyond description.

SOL DUC HOT SPRINGS

OSCAR PETERSON, *Guide*

1 Day Horseback Trips from Sol Duc Hot Springs

Place	Distance Round Trip Miles	Riding Time Round Trip Hours	Cost per Horse
Sol Duc Falls	6	2	$2.00
Mink Lake	6	2½	2.00
Low Divide	10	6	4.00
Blackwood Lake	12	7	4.50
Deer Lake	12	6	4.00
7 Lakes Basin	18	8	5.00
Bogachiel Peak	20	9	5.50
Hoh Lake	24	10	6.00
Sol Duc Park	20	9	5.50
Appleton Peak	20	9	6.00

Other Trips, Including Guide, Meals, Tents, Bedding, Saddle Horse

	Distance Round Trip	Days	Cost per Day per Person
Head of Cat Creek	26	2 or longer	$9.00
Olympus Ranger Station	34	2 or longer	9.00
Jackson Station	52	3 or longer	9.00
Blue Glacier and Mt. Olympus	60	5 or longer	9.00
Bogachiel River	42	3 or longer	9.00

Horses by the hour—$1.00, or $6.00 by the day.

Sights on Trails

300 miles government trails.
350 varieties of wild flowers.
Mountain Marmonts, deer, elk, bear, other wild game.
Mountain peaks, glaciers, mountain lakes, virgin timber, fishing.
See ocean from Bogachiel Peak on a clear day.

Oscar Peterson at Sol Duc - late twenties

The resignation of Ranger Morganroth, effective December 31, 1927, and the subsequent hiring of Sanford Floe, proved to be a turning point for the Petersons. Ranger Floe appreciated Oscar's woodsman skill as well as his good humor under the most adverse circumstances. Oscar had the skills of the nineteenth century mountain man. His expertise was indispensable in the last American wilderness. Sanford moved to change Oscar's work status from contractor to employee. Although the Peterson pantry* suffered mightily from this turn of events, the bank account did not. This employment meant a regular paycheck and it was especially valued during the financially dismal 1930′s.

Another resignation occurred early in 1927 and proved pivotal in Minnie's life. The cook for the highway engineers at Nolan Creek quit. Working conditions were not quite what Cookie had envisioned when he signed on. The pay was good but hardly adequate compensation to offset the discomforts of life in a tent twenty miles from town. Cookie had also heard cougars were thick in the Hoh Valley. Graphic tales of these ferocious predators filled the crews' conversation and fueled Cookie's nightmares. Especially bothersome was the story of a Vancouver Island boy who had been eaten the year before. Cookie's near obsession with the topic impaired his performance as camp cook to the point of jeopardizing his job.

Then he saw his first cougar and when Ira Otis met Oscar the following day he was looking for a cook. "No," he didn't know anyone except maybe Minnie, who had cooked for her father's construction crew. Oscar assured Ira that Minnie had no fear of cougars and in April, 1927 Minnie packed up Oscar Jr. and eleven month old Carma and headed south to Nolan Creek on horseback. The work was not the most pleasant but the job meant she had her own money** and another measure of independence.

---

*   Oscar's hunting habits were strictly by the book after he became a USFS employee.
**   In 1927 Minnie made her first property purchase in the Hoh Valley.

Minnie's first purchase of Hoh real estate - 1927
Sixty - acre homestead on the Upper Hoh

Minnie's kitchen at Nolan Creek - 1927

Oscar Jr.'s playground - 1927

Ben and Myrtle Walking visit Minnie at Nolan Creek - 1927
A welcomed break.

Sand bar at Nolan Creek - 1927
Minnie, unknown, Myrtle

Minnie and Oscar at Jackson Ranger Station - mid twenties.

While Minnie cooked, Oscar packed. The country was in the midst of the roaring twenties and Oscar's 1927 bookings filled up nicely. In fact, the time came when logistical considerations demanded the services of another packer. Over the early years of their marriage, Minnie had always been eager to accept invitations to ride along and help Oscar. She was a quick study and had learned to balance packs and tie the diamond hitch.* Oscar explained his predicament and asked her to help for a few days.** Minnie took little convincing. Nolan Creek had meant heat, cold, bugs, mud and vermin and these adversities had taken their toll as is chronicled in this letter to Oscar.

July 23, 1927
Dear Oscar—

I got your letter this afternoon. It's so hot here today I am almost melting. You are pretty wise going to the hot springs where you can have a bath every day and play with the pretty girls in the pool. Mr. Otis told me the other day that chances are, that we will be moving to Forks in a few weeks. You don't need to say anything to any body as he isn't sure yet. If we move to Forks we will be camped at the end of the road. I was so happy thinking I might see you often then but now that you are going to the hot springs it won't make any difference where we are camped. This is good haying weather. Only it's a little too hot in the tent for real comfort. We have two new records now—one is sure a comical one. It's one that I'm sure you will like. The mosquitoes are terrible here both in the evenings and mornings. Carma is cutting some of her double teeth now so she is a little cross. I got a full crew to cook for now so am kept busy. Hoping to see you in a few days.

With love,
Minnie

---

*   Diamond hitch: the complex knot that keeps the pack on a horse.
**   "a few days" turned into 50 years

Minnie's Apprenticeship
Hoh Valley - mid twenties

Jackson Ranger Station - mid twenties

DEPARTMENT OF PREPARATION
JAMES L. CLARK, ASSISTANT TO THE DIRECTOR
IN FULL CHARGE OF PREPARATION

May 12 1924.

My Dear Oscar:

Well old top how are you and all you family and all the long tails and big horns up the river?

I was over to the Explorers Club of which I am a member and saw the Dr. and he told me that he would be with you this fall. Well Oscar I am glad that you made connections for when he saw the lecture I gave at the club here last winter and I told them all about the glories and wonders of the Olympics and showed the pistures he came to me and wanted to know if he could get you for his guide. So you see old timer I have spread your fame from coast to coast.

I also havea surprise for you ----for I am coming to the coast in a little over a month and get a new sea lion group. Hurrah! I told the Dr. that I would see you before he would when I saw him at the Club Friday night.

I condemned the group of Sea Lions that they just paid $1500 for last year. It rather surprised them but they backed me with the money to get another group on the coast. So now Old top, when I get out there Ill also have 3 weeks vacation after I wind up with the sea lions and I would just be tickled pink if Minnie Carma you and I could run up to the divide for a little while.

I am having a hum dinger of a new motion picture made especially for me and I am anxious to try it out on Elk. Ill have a lens on it so that the elk will look life size from where we took them lying down last year. I can now take them 6 times farther away than I could before and still make them as large.

Now Oscar I want you to write me at once---if you possiblycan get off about the middle of July or a little later and still be back to take out the Dr, I dont know when you do your haying. I supposethat it will be your busy season. I am sure that this will be the last time for a long --long time that we will be together and so we ought to have a hell of a time, If you are still packing up in there for the fire patrol we might go in with you and get some one else go out with.Even if you couldnt stayl long with us, Minnie Carma an I could chase around. I am sure Minnie could go as I remember that she said she never got tired of the out doors.This will also give Carma a chance for atrip that she missed last year. Think up some plan Oscar and write me at once. You know it takes a long time for the mail to go between us.

I will also bring my motion pictures that I took last year and we can have them shown at he Forks show,wont that be a treat? You will also see Glen Merchant with his whiskers.

I also want to take in a dance or two while I am in your neck of the woods. I plan to be at the beach after sea lionsfor at least 3 weeks and can run up in between times ad see you,so all told we ought to have a royal time.

This ought to put me in your neighborhood around the 4th and there will sure be a celebration some where.

I would like to stay up in the Taft creek region for a week and then hike up to the top for some more Mt. stuff and and then out again with out going clear around as we did last year. I think the best stuff is on the Hoh side.

Well hoping to hear from you soon I am ,

Yoursfor a good time.

C. J. Albrecht

Write me to the address on the envelop,

Best regards to all.
May be Teoval would like to go along.
He might find some more Diamonds.

56

Journeyman and apprentice on the High Divide
Oscar in the middle, Minnie on the right

Minnie was clearly ready for a career change. She started by packing for the trail crew while Oscar guided a private party. Minnie and Oscar teamed up for the hunting season and together guided to the Deer Lake and the Upper Bogachiel areas.

Minnie comes to the rescue - August 1927
from original photo:
"Minnie and Oscar
left to right - Jiggo, Ranger, Babe, Bosco"

CHAPTER FOUR

HOME AWAY FROM HOME

Spring days in 1928 were filled with the usual farm and domestic chores. Though Minnie's hands were busy, her mind was fully occupied with plans for the coming summer. There was much to be done in preparation. Vivian (12), Ivan (11), Oscar (6), and Carma (2) needed supervision she would not be able to provide. Minnie talked to Oscar's mother, his Aunt Flora, and her own parents, and arranged a complicated and creative scheme of child care that allowed the older children to be with her at Sol Duc whenever possible.* Her next challenge was C.F. Martin, owner of Sol Duc. She needed to rent the farm below the hot springs from him as well as deal with a few loose ends left by Oscar and his brother Morton. The loose ends had to do with the fact that while Minnie's brother, Sheriff Bill Nelson, and his successors had taken on the task of smashing every still in Clallam County, Morton, and to a lesser extent his brother Oscar, were doing their best to make sure the moon shiners thrived.

Minnie rented the farm and assured C.F. Martin that management would be tightened. If Minnie was to be a regular on USFS trails she had one other person to deal with and that was Ranger Floe. Fortunately, Minnie had an advocate. Esther, the Ranger's wife, was generous in her praise of Minnie.** By this time Oscar's word also carried weight with Ranger Floe. The first decent day in June 1928, Minnie moved the horses to Sol Duc and set about making the small cabin below the springs livable. Her horses enjoyed the comforts of a barn across the yard and nice pasture another mile down river at the Jones homestead.

Oscar Jr. at daycare, Sol Duc style - 1927

---

*   Pete remembers spending his days in the Sol Duc pool starting at six years old. At WSC he was on the swim team and later taught swimming in the Army.
** Esther was a fellow horsewoman who over the years often rode with Minnie and became a friend and confidant for life. They were often mistaken for each other since they were of similar build.

Grandparents and daycare providers - 1928
Oscar, Ivan, Sophie, Carma, Oscar Jr., Nels, Vivian

Barn at Sol Duc
Oscar Sr. and son, Pete

Minnie's cabin on the farm below Sol Duc
Courtesy of Olympic National Park

The resort itself was about one-half mile up river from her cabin. At the upstream end of the grounds was a large pool. Adjacent to it down river was a smaller pool covered by an extension of the hotel roof. Posts came out of the middle of the pool to support the roof. In the basement level of the hotel were dressing rooms for the pool and private rooms for mineral baths and massages. From the hotel porch on the side opposite the covered pool, guests could survey the rest of the grounds. On the left, a building was home to a store, café and dining room. Gas was available in front of the store. Just a little downstream from the gas pumps in roughly the middle of the grounds and across from the entrance was a large rectangular open space, the site of the glorious old Sol Duc Hotel.

On either side of this space were cabins. Across the entrance bridge and down river was the hub of social activity at Sol Duc - the dance hall. Back on the Hot Springs side of the bridge and farther yet down the river was a covered picnicking area and to the left of it, tennis courts. Further uphill and away from the river were the fresh ashes of the second Sol Duc Hotel.

Just beyond the second hotel site, conveniently located near the Mink Lake trail head, was Minnie's place of business. She kept her horses here on the days she was not in the back country or picking up day rides. Minnie posted her offerings and rates* at the Sol Duc Store.

There were never enough of the longer trips for Minnie. When she felt the need, she headed for the high country, clients or not. Sometimes she rode alone and sometimes Esther Floe, Mickey Merchant or other friends accompanied her. Fortunately, neither Sanford nor Oscar was the jealous type.

Later in that summer of 1928 Minnie got her wish for a really long backcountry adventure, her first expedition style pack trip.** In the course of two weeks, Minnie and her party retraced the Press Expedition's route taken thirty years earlier. They traveled up the

Sol Duc -1930

---

*   Later during the depression Minnie offered 25 cent rides commensurate with people's reduced discretionary funds.

**   Documentation for this trip is sparse except for the fact that in 1977 she repeated the route and called it a fifty year anniversary trip. The year 1927 seems improbable for a number of reasons, one of which is her lack of experience at that point.

Elwha, past Lost Cabin Mountain, across the Lillian River by Mount Scott and into the Press Valley, by Mount Dana and Wilder, and then across Godkin Creek, through Marmot Pass and to the Low Divide under Mount Seattle. They rode off the Low Divide into the Quinault Valley and then to Lake Quinault.

The route north to Forks from Lake Quinault was being widened and in some cases entirely rerouted to accommodate a new stretch of Highway 101. As Minnie turned her horses north she was more than anxious to get home. She became tired of the endless coastal swamps. Minnie's clients sensed this and thus it was with some trepidation that they asked politely for a rest and picture break. Minnie brought her lead horse to a halt and swung out of the saddle. This text would have been short indeed if she had pushed ahead any further. No sooner had she tied her horse than she heard a distant call, "Fire in the hole!" Pulling her clients behind trees, they watched in dismay as the ground convulsed and the trail ahead turned into a wall of flying rock, mud and chunks of wood. The horses tested their halters and diamond hitches as rocks rained down through the branches of the big spruce next to the right of way. As thunderous as it was, this blast was a small pop compared to the explosion that followed.

Minnie knew that the required watchman had not been at his post. She also knew who was ultimately responsible for the near miss - the blaster in charge. It is clear to all those who have been dressed down by Minnie that, had the blaster in charge been allowed a choice that day, he would have certainly preferred corporal punishment over Minnie's verbal onslaught. On a scale of one to ten, where the wrath of God is ten, Minnie, as a thirty-year-old woman, could reach the nines. She was in the high nines that day.*

Sometime later, Minnie's clients and horses arrived back in Forks glad for the trip but also glad to be out of the back country. Oscar was familiar with the Press Expedition route from his trips in the 1910's and early twenties and he knew that if Minnie could make that trip, the rest of the Olympics could certainly be hers.

View of Sol Duc Hot Springs - 1930
Dance Hall - upper center, Store - lower left, Pools - out of view to the right

---

* As teenagers, Minnie's grandchildren figured that the Washington correctional system could be dismantled by substituting jail time for short conversations with Minnie, wherein the convicts would be shown the error of their ways.

Chapter Five

Twenties end with a crash and a fire.

The 1929 hunting season had ended in the Upper Sol Duc. Minnie's horses were out of the high country and the saddle gear oiled and stored in the back room of the resort's dance hall. When the day late newspaper arrived on October 30th, it brought news of the stock market collapse. Oscar's idea of an investment had been wildcat wells or gold claims, so they lost no money in the market. On the other hand, rich folks from Seattle who had come to Sol Duc in increasing numbers during the roaring twenties, many driving big new cars, were not so lucky. Most of those folks lost money and lots of it.

Minnie, who was often captivated by the wit and humor of her favorite American media star, Will Rogers, was not amused by the ramifications of his report from Wall Street: "You have to stand in line to get a window to jump out of."

Would there be a tourist season in 1930? The question was nearly moot when tragedy struck a third time at Sol Duc. Two elegant hotels had gone up in flames in previous years, this time it was the dance hall. It would be rebuilt; it was central to the Sol Duc experience. But this time Minnie had lost her tack. All of the riding saddles, pack saddles, bridles, tarps and sling ropes that Oscar had collected over the years, were gone. There remained one good bridle and saddle and the halters Minnie had used to string the horses on the trip home that fall.

Oscar went to work that winter. Discarded saddles were resurrected; sawbuck saddles for packing were carved and fitted with breast straps and briching.* Some of it wasn't pretty but it worked.

---

*   Breast straps keep the load from slipping over the horse's rear, while briching keeps the load from going over the horse's head.

7-30-36   L. MOE   I.R.   918 BOGACHIEL PEAK

The twenties had been good to Minnie and Oscar. By 1928 Minnie's employment, the Highway 101 construction project, the USFS work and the private trips had contributed enough to allow the couple to buy a new car, fancy riding outfits, chaps, shirts, breeches and sombreros for both. In spite of the news of the stock market collapse, Minnie rejoiced at their good fortune. "If we had waited another year we would not have been able to buy these things."

Minnie returned to Sol Duc in 1930 hoping for the best. The outlook, however, was bleak and the worst of it was that the family had begun to depend on Minnie's income. No one seemed to have much money but by June the cabins at Sol Duc began to fill up. Loyal Seattleites with family traditions returned and Finns from Grays Harbor, who could not get through a year without their annual trip to the baths at Sol Duc, came back.

Henry David Thoreau wrote "I frequently tramped eight or ten miles through the deepest snow to keep an appointment with a beech tree or yellow birch or an old acquaintance among the pines." Like Thoreau years before, by 1930 Minnie had come under the beckoning power of the high country wilderness; she was under its spell. Furthermore, she felt comfortable riding the steep snowy meadows and ravines on her sure-footed mountain pony.

Her first reconnaissance ride in 1930 was all about renewing acquaintances and revisiting friends. She drank in the sights and sounds of the landscape, the thunderous Sol Duc Falls in all its glory, the recently thawed Deer Lake with this year's crop of trout rising to its surface, the snowy ridge above the lake, her campsite on this ridge. As usual the elk were there to greet Minnie in the Bogachiel head-waters. They frolicked on a snowfield below and stopped their play only long enough to identify the sound of the horse's steel shoes on stone.

Below - 360° panoramic from Bogachiel Peak - Cougar Fields collection

Farther up the trail the Rock Hollow was covered by snow, as could be expected this time of year. Here Minnie tied her horse and walked to the Seven Lake Basin Overlook. The upper lakes were still frozen and a mantle of snow lingered on the northern exposures. On up the trail the switch backs defied gravity, appearing suspended above the Bogachiel Valley. Not a place for the acrophobic. Looking straight down a one thousand foot cliff from the back of a horse as it carefully maneuvers along a one foot wide trail, tends to focus one's attention on the frailty of life.

Minnie knew her horse Bosco and her attention was on another herd of elk on the far side of the valley. Bosco rounded the final turn and Minnie made a mental note, "Must tell the Ranger these trail turnouts need work." Up ahead loomed Bogachiel Peak. Minnie tied her sweaty horse and scrambled up a set of switch-backs positioned on an extreme piece of Olympic real estate. Minnie had made this trip many times by now but could never quite prepare herself for this place. Like approaching royalty, it was something you did not get used to. Sitting down for a lunch of hardtack, cheese, and dried fruit, Minnie surveyed the scene before her. Chris Morganroth described it best in his autobiography:

The Rock Hollow - looking toward Bogachiel Peak

GACHIEL PEAK   MT. OLYMPUS   30-36   L. MOE   I. R.

Looking south not over six miles away, across what had to be the immense Hoh River Valley, was mighty Mount Olympus. To the east was a range of mountain peaks. Still farther to the east and southeast lay a jumble of snow-covered peaks, glaciers and large snow fields. Facing north and directly below us lay the huge peaceful basin where we had camped the night before. It appeared to be about two miles wide and a thousand to fifteen hundred feet deep. The floor of the basin was covered with loose slide rock from the surrounding high rim. Low hillocks and ridges lay within the basin with scattered clusters of stunted alpine trees on them. This natural amphitheater could easily seat a million spectators. Looking beyond the basin to the northeast were several snow capped peaks, some with glaciers. To the west, some forty miles distance we could see the Pacific Ocean with a tiny ship far out at sea. We turned and faced Mt. Olympus again, this time observing it as a backdrop for the heavily forested Hoh Valley, which lay between us and the mountain. The Hoh River could be seen threading its way through the dense forest like a silver ribbon on its way to the sea.

Chris Morganroth had been here first in 1892. Not much had changed in thirty-eight years. Minnie took one last look, wandered down the trail toward Bosco, mounted the anxious horse and headed for the barn at Sol Duc. All was well on the High Divide.

Meanwhile, back at the Hot Springs, Minnie had a little competition. C.F. Martin, not one to miss much, had calculated what half hour rides were adding up to for Minnie. He promptly went out and bought an adorable Shetland pony with the idea of increasing resort profits as well as recreational offerings. The pony had other ideas. Buster the pony turned out to be a cute, uncooperative little Shetland with a rather long list of unpleasant habits. Somewhere near the top of this list was his inclination to bite the adoring, but unsuspecting, in the britches. C.F. soon realized that bruises on backsides were not a good advertisement for Sol Duc and handling this creature was beyond the scope of the Sol Duc crew. This pony seemed to be a one person horse and that person was Minnie's son, Oscar Jr. (Pete). C.F. gave the horse to him.

At age nine Pete entered the business world by offering rides, one trip around the old hotel site for five cents and a fifteen minute ride for twenty-five cents. The horseback rides had limited entertainment value, however, since the scenery really didn't change during the ride and, although the rider got to hold the reins, Pete kept a firm grip on the horse´s halter rope.

917 BOGACHIEL PEAK   MT. OLYMPUS N.M.

Oscar Jr. (Pete) and Buster at Sol Duc - 1931
Hibben and Bole photo

CHAPTER SIX

THE JUGGLING ACT: FARM, FAMILY, FOREST

On August 16, 1930 Minnie picked up the *Port Angeles Evening News* and was horrified by the lead article titled, "Proposal Made for Scenic Route to High Places." If the Peninsula and Port Angeles Chambers of Commerce had their way, her fledgling outfitting business would die before it left the ground. Chris Morganroth and local business leaders were proposing to replace the trail system connecting the Elwha, Sol Duc, and the Hoh with a system of roads that would allow auto traffic across the High Divide to within a stone's throw of Blue and White glaciers.

By the first week of September, Chris had recruited H. Van Brocklin of the Port Angeles Chamber, A. Carter and W. Spooner of the Forks Commercial Club, H.W. Davies, engineer for Port of Port Angeles, A.J. Hartzler, H. Beetle, O. Harris, M. Schmidt, D. Lutz, J. Hensen, G. Ustler and K. Knutsen, for an overnight trip over much of the proposed route.

All together the party that left Sol Duc Hot Springs at 8 a.m. Sunday morning consisted of thirteen civic representatives as well as Oscar Peterson and nine pack and saddle horses. The group returned to Sol Duc the following day and in the September 9, 1930 *Port Angeles Evening News*, the route was declared feasible and its praises sung in fifty column inches. The whole idea made Minnie sick at her stomach.*

Although the stock market crash had caused people to be just a little tighter with their depreciating funds, overall the year 1930 had been passable for Minnie at Sol Duc. At the end of the season, however, Minnie's saddle bags were lighter than she had hoped.

Minnie's ride home from Sol Duc took her through the little community of Beaver, the same afternoon as the annual turkey shoot. The loud noises agitated the horses but Minnie was anxious to join the fun and after tying them securely, she raced off to enter the competition. By the time the shooting ended, Minnie had in her possession eleven turkeys, a rifle given to her by a thoroughly defeated and disgusted competitor, and somewhat fuller saddle bags from side bets.** No witnesses are left to tell, but anyone who ever watched Minnie in action knows what she had to say each time she pulled the trigger. "Aren't I lucky?"

Minnie in full dress uniform

---

*   Happily for Minnie, soon National Monument and later National Park status precluded the execution of this plan.
**   Minnie put the live turkeys in bags on the horses.

Main Street Forks - scene of the annual Peterson cattle drive

The first order of ranching business in the spring of 1931 was the annual cattle drive to the Hoko Homestead. This had been done uneventfully right through the center of Forks for many years but those had been the years before Oscar and Minnie acquired Hector the bull. Hector was quiet enough around people in the barn and pasture. What did annoy Hector to an extreme degree was the thought of competition and that was exactly what Hector saw in the window of Mr. Goss's Drug Store in downtown Forks the day of the drive. Unexpectedly and to Oscar and Minnie's utter dismay, Hector made a run at the other bull and only hesitated when he realized that the bull on the other side of the plate glass was just as mean looking as himself with the same steam coming from his nostrils. As Minnie watched from the back of her cow pony she visualized the amount of mayhem and destruction a 2000 pound bull could cause in a 1500 square foot retail space.

A second run at the window was thwarted when son Ivan, at Minnie's urging, made a desperate move to distract Hector. Ivan was only successful because, from Hectors new vantage point, the bull in the store front had disappeared. The Peterson fortunes had been saved from a considerable setback.

In the meantime, over on the Hoko River homestead, the rats had pillaged some very valuable packing gear and chewed up considerable latigo leather strap. Minnie was fit to be tied. Oscar thought it was funny till the following morning when he found that the longest piece of shoelace he had to tie his boots was about three inches long. Fortunately, Oscar never let a run of bad luck get him down.

This was especially true later in the spring of 1931. Oscar had no sooner recovered from the indignity of the rats when his fortunes went further south in the annual "Minnie and Bosco versus Oscar and Bay Bill" horse race. After the financial losses of this incident, Oscar was looking for a sure bet and figured he had found it in his fourteen-year-old son. He made a double or nothing wager in the race he arranged between Minnie and Ivan. Oscar bet on Ivan, of course, because he was faster. He lost the bet, of course, because Minnie was more sure footed and lucky. Ivan slipped and fell at the start.* **

---

*   Oscar Jr. had to learn the hard way just how lucky Minnie was. In 1932 Pete lost a calf to Minnie over the outcome of a middle weight prize fight that took place in Seattle. Fifty years later Pete was reminded of this miscalculation as he flipped coins with Minnie to see who paid for dinner on a road trip to the Grand Canyon. Minnie had only one thing to say each time she defied the law of averages and Pete paid for another meal, "Aren't I lucky?" Oscar Jr. came home from the army with all his wages because of these lessons.

**   In later years she rarely collected winnings but kept running tallies close at hand for whenever a player might return.

Oscar and Bay Bill, Minnie and Bosco - 1931
Hibben and Bole photo

The year 1931 shaped up early to be busy as Minnie and Oscar diligently pursued promising new possibilities to enhance their business. In a March 25, 1931 letter to Ranger Floe, Oscar and Minnie proposed a cabin on the ridge* above Deer Lake. Letters were then exchanged with Olympic National Forest Supervisor Plumb. His response was positive with the only point of contention being placement.

Oscar and Minnie wanted the cabin accessible early in the season which is what the site above Deer Lake would accomplish. Supervisor Plumb liked the High Divide where the views were better, but the Petersons figured the late snow, water and horse feed, might be a problem. In the middle of this discussion, a letter that changed everything came from the Cleveland Museum of Natural History. A full blown expedition of the Peninsula's western and central interior was being proposed by the museum. Oscar sent his resume and bid price by return mail May 25, 1931. This would be Oscar's first big outing in years and he was ready. In a May 31, 1931 letter, B.P. Bole accepted Oscar's terms. Final arrangements were made for a start date on about July 1st.

THE CLEVELAND MUSEUM OF NATURAL HISTORY

TWENTY-SEVEN SEVENTEEN EUCLID AVENUE

CLEVELAND

May 31 1931

Mr. Oscar Peterson,
Forks,
Clallam Co.,
Washington.

Dear Mr. Peterson:-

You letter of May 25 is received.

I was very glad to see that you have been on other collecting expeditions before, particularly with people of national reputation. Your prices, moreover, are very satisfactory. I see by your letter that you have received $40 a month for each of your pack horses, excluding the one that is included in your own salary. In my last letter to you I said that we would be out for three weeks, but since writing you I have decided to remain in the field at least one month, or thirty days. We will select you as our packer if you will accept $50 a month for each horse other than the one you ride; that is, fifty dollars per horse for the first thirty days and $2.50 a day per horse for each day over that number that we are on the trip. You yourself would get $6.00 a day throughout. If this is agreeable to you, we will start out on or very soon after July 1.

We will have with us two collecting cases. These are wooden frames that fit into two small trunks, the trunks being about 28" long, 15 " wide, and 9 " deep. They are not very heavy. If you think it would be easier for you, I can have leather loops put on that would fit over the trees of the packsaddles like a regular pack. I suppose, however, that you are like most other packers and like diamond hitches best. In all, I suppose we shall need four horses other than the one you ride. Mr. Hibben and I will walk, as we shall do some collecting while moving from camp to camp.

There are a few questions that I would like to hear from you about pretty soon. These are: Can we express stuff direct to wherever your outfit is? Also, where is your outfit, at Soleduck Park or at Forks?

Hoping that the above suggestions as to prices, etc., will be all right with you, I am

Yours truly,

B. P. Bole jr.

Ass't in Charge of Mammalogy

---

*   Later to be named Minnie Peterson Ridge.

Oscar and Minnie went to work figuring out how they were going to pull this off logistically. Obvious to both of them was the fact that Minnie, for the first time, would be on her own. Fortunately, most of what Oscar had taught her over the years had become second nature. Minnie knew that if she treated the horses right and considered their needs first, they would return the favor and not let her down. The horses varied from beautiful to down right ugly. Their personalities varied as much as their looks, from friendly to indifferent to obnoxious but they were all sure-footed and hard workers. Minnie knew that if the horses had confidence in her they would go anywhere and do anything for her. (*Western Horseman* 1975)

Minnie goes solo, High Divide - 1931

Minnie poses with visitors to Sol Duc - 1931

Day trip on the Sol Duc loop - 1931

Vivian

Ivan, Carma, and kitten, the one not having a good time

Minnie's children pose for Frank Hibben in front of Sol Duc cabin - 1931
Hibben and Bole photos

Minnie at the terminus of the Blue after safe negotiation of the bluff

Oscar also had confidence in Minnie but there was one stretch of "trail" that had him worried-the shale cliff below Glacier Meadows.* She understood that her credibility as a packer depended on her ability to make this passage safely. This bluff was covered with fine loose rock that continually migrated down slope so obstacles had to be removed every time this dangerous traverse was attempted. Oscar was very firm about this explaining that once out on the precipice the horses could not be turned around. This also meant that Minnie had to establish definitively that no pack train would be passing from the opposite direction. Oscar also explained in detail where the horses could be safely tied so that Minnie could check the route and make any necessary repairs. (*There Was a Day*)

So it was that in the summer of 1931 Oscar set off on the trip of a lifetime with two young scientists, Pat Bole and Frank Hibben** and Minnie established herself as a packer and guide in her own right.

---

*　Historically few people crossed the bluff with horses. Now none do.

**　Hibben´s career was as notable as it was long. In 1931 Hibben was just 20 years old. By 1937 he had earned a Masters in Zoology and a Ph.D. in archaeology. The Ph.D. from Harvard took him one year. During WWII his job was to take battle plans, only in his mind, from the joint chiefs to war theaters around the world. Later in the war his plane was shot down by a German submarine. After the war, he created the Museum of Anthropology at the University of New Mexico, worked with Louis and Mary Leakey in Africa, served as a secret agent for friend President Richard Nixon, wrote numerous books and hundreds of articles and before his death in 2002, funded the Hibben Center UNM, which serves as the home for the ten million dollar Hibben Trust.

Minnie says goodbye to the explorers July 1931 at Sol Duc cabin.
Left to right: Oscar, Minnie, Pat Bole - Hibben and Bole photo

Posturing for the camera - High Divide 1931
Hibben and Bole photo

Camp at Glacier Meadows - Cleveland Museum Expedition 1931
Frank Hibben and Oscar - Hibben and Bole photo

Hibben's first bear
Hibben and Bole photo

Camp at south Kimta Basin - July 26, 1931
Hibben and Bole photo

"Pat" and Mother Bessie with Oscar 1931
Hibben and Bole photo

"Pat negotiating the Clearwater River behind his mother Bessie" - July 31, 1931
Hibben and Bole photo

"The three tramps" back at Forks - 1931
Left to right: Pat, Oscar, Frank - Hibben and Bole photo

The 1931 packing season passed quickly. Unfortunately, in the fall of 1931, a year after she had "cleaned house," Minnie was no longer welcome at the Beaver Turkey shoot. Minnie was "lucky" though, because the fowl on the Peterson farm had been busy all spring and the ranch was benefiting from a considerable surplus of geese, ducks and chickens.

Shortly after Minnie returned from the mountains that fall, Oscar built a huge cage for the back of their pickup truck. The couple recruited a friend, Micky Merchant, to handle side bets and run a craps game for those who figured they were better off in a game of chance. The turkey shoot, sans turkeys, went off without a hitch. This was due in no small part to the fact that the deputy sheriff, the only law between Port Angeles and Hoquaim, was occupied by some out-of-town business.* The locals had not had this much fun since the last carnival. Minnie counted the receipts, paid the help and became even more convinced that, although she was an excellent shooter, her real talents were those of an entrepreneur.

---

*   There have been doubts raised as to whether the deputy cared judging from the other enterprises in Forks he chose to overlook.

THE CLEVELAND MUSEUM OF NATURAL HISTORY

TWENTY-SEVEN SEVENTEEN EUCLID AVENUE

CLEVELAND

Dear Oscar:- 												July 11 1934

I was tickled pink to get your swell letter.

Mother has officially given up her trip out your way
this year, because Dad couldn't get away and her friends backed
down also. She doesn't want to go out alone, so that's that.
I told you in my last letter that she might not get around to it
this year, but she may next, and her heart is so set on it I
know she'll do it sometime. Another reason why she didn't
want to leave this summer is because of my approaching marriage.

Your forest service job sounds swell to me and I'm
looking forward to hearing all the low-down you promised me.
I liked the snapshots of our Cakemaker and my namesake and I've
got them on my desk right this minute. I'd surely like to
come back to your stamping ground, Oscar---- the Olympics are
one of the best countries Frank and I have seen and we've seen
several since we were with you.

Our place in town here was all blown to bits yesterday
evening in a big blow-down. They had hailstones as big as eggs
and they just raised holy hell with the trees and windows and
gardens. One of our men's cars had its roof all punched full
of holes and some greenhouses nearby looked as though they had
been hit by shells. We had trees blown down all over, and
about three inches of rain in just nothing flat. Funny thing
about it was we only had a slight shower out at our farm, 20 miles
away, and no wind or hail.

I've heard nothing from Frank lately except that hE 's
going to be in New Mexico for sometime to come. I got that
from his cousin, one of 600 hens I had to lecture to a few days
ago. Oscar, you'ld have just loved to have been there. The woods
were full of them.

Don't forget that low-down you promised me, but for
the love of pete don't take time out to write me if you're rushed.

So long and good luck---

Pat

CHAPTER SEVEN

CINDY TAKES A TUMBLE

By the summer of 1932, paperwork for the proposed cabin above Deer Lake had been processed. Between Minnie's paying jobs and Oscar's USFS obligation, Minnie and Oscar began moving building materials to the construction site. Minnie had packed everything from dynamite to cook stoves but it was the sixteen foot lumber for this project that she always recalled causing her the worst, near catastrophe.

The pack string had crossed the bridge at Sol Duc Falls and was proceeding up toward Canyon Creek when one of the pack horse's loads of long boards struck a tree on a sharp corner. Cindy backed up to regain her balance, then pitched overboard, sliding and rolling, narrowly missing porcupine logs.* She came to an abrupt stop one hundred feet above the Sol Duc River, the lumber on her back lodged between two trees. She struggled, the cinch broke, and Minnie watched in horror as the pony fought in vain for footing on the vertical canyon wall, then tumbled down the precipice. Oscar scrambled down the slope expecting the worst and found Cindy motionless on her side. Minnie recounted for Will Muller, writing in the *Western Horseman* December 1975, what happened next,

"Come on Cindy, get up, Oscar commanded. Cindy got to her feet slowly and uncertainly, and she shook herself hard. She didn't even have a scratch."

Sol Duc Falls - scene of Cindy's close call (far right)

---

* These logs with short hard knots can often be fatal.

Minnie's completed cabin - Spring 1933

Oscar climbed out of the canyon and galloped back to Sol Duc for tools. By the time he returned with axe and grub hoe, Minnie had already begun digging a steep pathway out of the canyon. By noon they were back on the trail. When the snow came to the high country in 1932, a cozy cabin was nestled into the trees at the edge of a meadow overlooking the Bogachiel Valley. Minnie's dream had come true.

Clients and Minnie's cabin - Summer 1933

CHAPTER EIGHT
"Wasn't I Lucky?"

Midsummer 1933, 12-year-old Oscar Jr. was at Sol Duc with Minnie but Pete's main source of income, Buster the Shetland pony, was not. C. F. Martin had gotten into the habit of throwing coins into the pools at Sol Duc to entertain the children. Because of this, Pete's swimming improved dramatically. He did retrieve his share of the coins, but there was no certainty in this activity especially when bigger boys were in the pool. Pete needed Buster, but Buster had not been brought to Sol Duc with the rest of the string. If Pete were to stay liquid, he needed Buster. Pete had learned the ropes the previous summer. He knew the potential of his enterprise. Every day without Buster was a wasted opportunity. Regrettably, moving the horse didn't seem to be very high on Oscar Sr.´s priority list. Finally, Pete was assured Buster would be coming the following weekend, Sunday at the latest. There was no horse on Saturday.

On Sunday the family car pulled up to the front of the cabin. No trailer was attached. It would be a wasted week before Oscar was back. The future of Pete's business looked dim indeed, until he saw what he thought was the muzzle of a horse pushing against the glass of the Buick touring car's rear passenger window. It was Buster alright in the car and Pete's business was soon solvent again.*

In 1933, as had become her custom, Minnie stayed at Sol Duc through the deer hunting season. It is unclear why, but in early November 1933 Minnie opted to take the horses to her Hoh River Ranch for fall pasture via Deer Lake, the High Divide and Hoh Lake. The weather turned from an assault of sleet to a full-scale attack of snowfall as she approached the ridge above Deer Lake. Minnie bundled into her extra clothes, turned her shoulder into the stinging snow, and rode the next five miles into a howling blizzard. In the drifting snow high above the Bogachiel headwaters, up the barely visible seven hanging switchbacks and then across the flank of Bogachiel Peak, she rode. Minnie protected her face from the snow and wind and let Bosco find the way. Relieved to feel the horse begin the descent toward Hoh Lake, Minnie reflected on the fact that five thousand feet was too high for November. All the way down to the valley floor Minnie promised herself she wouldn't try that again. She didn't, and this story, like many, was always told with the cautionary punch line, "Wasn't I lucky?"

1950's photo of area Minnie traversed in the blizzard of 1933.
Photo by Alice Graham

---

*   Beyond their own enterprises, Pete and Ivan had family responsibilities. Every morning at five they had breakfast and then hiked to the Old Jones Homestead below Sol Duc where the horses were put to pasture every evening. If they weren't so lucky, the horses would be farther down in a second clearing. The boys carried only a halter and lead rope with them and after they caught a horse they galloped back, driving the rest of the horses ahead of them. The horses were then fed oats, wiped down, saddled up and walked to the Sol Duc resort.

By 1934 Pete and Ivan carried most of the farming load for Minnie and Oscar. After school was out the boys put up the neighbor's hay in exchange for the use of equipment to use for their own hay harvest. Grandmas, aunts, and uncles supervised the Peterson kids when they were free to do so, and Ivan, Vivian, Pete and Carma supervised themselves the rest of the time. Supervised or not, the Peterson household was a magnet for young people. All were welcome as long as they would help with the chores. Notable for the amount of time they spent on the Peterson ranch were Claude Clark and Junior Kruger. On one occasion Junior's parents retrieved him with the help of the town Marshal.

The fun at the Peterson place out-weighed the hard work and Minnie's occasional harshness. There was calf-riding, horseback riding, card playing, ice skating and hockey in the winters, mumbly peg,* wrestling, fireworks on the Fourth of July, and target shooting.

It has been previously noted that for Minnie and Oscar, the line between work and play was often blurred. This was especially true when dynamite was involved. Oscar had a simple solution to almost any problem. That solution was dynamite, and the bigger the problem, the more dynamite was required. Oscar reasoned that it was a waste of time working up a sweat moving logs, rock, earth or stumps when you had dynamite on hand. Oscar always had plenty, thanks to the USFS.**

---

*   Mumbly peg is a pocket knife flicking game with points awarded for how the knife lands.
**   Leftover powder could not be stored safely over the winter and had to be disposed of every fall.

In 1934 quite a bit of dynamite had been left over from summer work and this made Oscar a happy man because it was going to take a lot to dig a garbage pit of the dimensions he envisioned. Oscar counted out 300 sticks from one half dozen partially filled boxes and calculated this to be precisely the correct amount for the job. He hitched Ranger to a sled. Ivan and Pete loaded the explosives aboard and up the hill they went to a point about 300 yards from the house.

About one half hour later, in the words of more than one local, "all hell broke loose." This time, Oscar and the boys were the lucky ones. That is, they were lucky Minnie was still in the back country and never saw the mess made by her fine china as it catapulted off the dining room plate rail. The clean up had barely gotten underway in the Peterson house when Claude Clark arrived carrying news from town, and wanting to see what things looked like closer to ground zero.

The news he brought was not good, mostly having to do with broken glass in and around the restaurants and bars. Much of the real damage, however, was not apparent that first evening. Roy Anderson's chicken ranch had sustained no physical damage but it seems his hens had suffered serious psychological harm. Roy's egg production was reduced to nothing overnight.

Ranger on fire wood gathering duty - 1933

Meanwhile, in the back country Minnie had her hands full. With Micky Merchant's help, Minnie was packing camp supplies and building materials for the lookout being built by Chris Morganroth and Charlie Anderson* at the summit of Bogachiel Peak. The contract called for Minnie to keep a construction camp supplied for six weeks and pack building materials to the lookout site. Tools, nails, lumber, windows, tents, blankets and food, all went up the mountain on Minnie's horses. The work started September 16th. (*Footprints in the Olympics*)

Things went smoothly enough at first but mid-September can be dangerously close to the time Pacific storms blow up through the Hoh Valley. By the third week in October monsoon season in the western Olympics was underway. Midway through that week Minnie and Micky Merchant ran out of daylight on their supply trip to Sol Duc.

---

* June 1933 brought change in the management of Mount Olympus Monument in the heart of the Olympics. Supervision was moved from the Agriculture Department to the Department of the Interior. Major O.A. Tomilson from Mount Rainier National Park was in charge. Chris had been recently employed by the National Park Service to do guiding and project work. He always argued for a national park so that recreation and scenery could be sold over and over again and it would still be there to pass on to future generations.

Micky Merchant packed up for Bogachiel Peak fire lookout construction project. Deer Lake - September 1934

Partially completed Bogachiel Peak lookout - September 1934

Minnie was not happy. Aware that horse, darkness, and the steep trail below Deer Lake in a storm, was not a safe mix, she opted to spend the night at the Deer Lake shelter. Late in the evening the full fury of the storm struck. The wind howled and the heavy cold rain, mixed with sleet, hail and wet snow pounded the shelter roof. While Minnie started breakfast the following morning Micky walked to the meadow above the lake to catch the horses.

This meadow was known for its pot holes that were evenly distributed around the area. Filled with snow melt from high in the basin, these holes were two to six feet deep, six to ten feet in diameter and had soft muddy bottoms and equally muddy perimeters. As Micky entered the meadow he strained to see through the storm to the commotion at its far end. From a distance it looked like trouble. He was right. Ranger was eyeball deep in one of the larger potholes, frantically trying to keep his nostrils out of the black brew he had stirred up. Micky ran back to camp, interrupted Minnie's breakfast preparation, and together they threw a pack saddle on their biggest mare.

Grabbing a bundle of rope they headed back to the meadow where Minnie threw a line over Micky and gave him a second to secure to Ranger's halter. Minnie tied Ranger's lead to the pack saddle and the big mare began to pull. Her heavy, sharp shod hooves bit deep into the wet turf. The leather of her breast strap stretched dangerously as Ranger slid slowly out of the hole.* Afterwards, Micky emerged. Caked with mud from head to foot, he looked like some swamp monster. After Ranger was wiped down and covered, Micky jumped into Deer Lake, clothes and all. He came out cleaner, but cold, wet and exhausted. Over the roar of the unrelenting storm, Micky proclaimed, "This weather might be alright for women and children but it is not tolerable for men and horses." ** Ranger returned to work and within a week the Bogachiel lookout was complete and ready for service.***

What Ranger lacked in intelligence he more than made up for in obedience and trust. Oscar Jr., always the showman, trained him to walk a plank and lay down on command, as well as a variety of other tricks. However, during the fall of 1934, Ranger gave Pete quite a scare. After impressing a group of admiring spectators in front of the Forks drug store with the "lay down" trick, Ranger failed on the "get up" part. Not surprising, the crowd really started to gather. Most were convinced this was no trick and the horse was sick. He wasn't. Ranger was just teasing. He finally got up and Pete rode him home.

Fall of the same year Oscar treated himself to a new pair of lace-to-the-knees work and riding boots. This was quite an investment for Oscar (the better part of a month's wages) but they would last if he took good care of them. Oscar brought the boots home, proudly showed them to Minnie and then went right to work lovingly massaging boot grease into the leather and carefully working it into all the seams. Oscar then set the boots next to the wood stove to dry but soon grew impatient with their progress and put them in the oven for just a little bit. An hour later the smell of toasting shoe leather reminded Oscar where they were. The next day when Pete asked him about his new boots, Oscar replied that he had cooked them in the wood stove but it was alright since buying another pair of boots was exactly what was needed to keep the shoe factories running during the hard times.

---

*   As grandchildren observing Minnie in similar circumstances, it seemed that she was able to will success in the most impossible circumstances.

**   Micky's slightly twisted exclamation has been repeated by Peterson men for over 65 years.

***   Minnie was relieved since this light workhorse was Oscar's pet.

Completed Bogachiel Peak Lookout

CHAPTER TEN
1937 HOH VALLEY MASSACRE

The elk season of 1937 brought hunters from all over the West Coast. Those who had never fired a rifle before bought out the local hardware stores of guns, ammunition, red shirts, and hats. They also bought out the Forks Liquor Store.* In an interview with Murray Morgan (*The Last Wilderness*), Minnie described what opening day sounded like from her vantage point in the sub-alpine country above the Hoh. It was like a battle or a western. "You'd hear a shot, then a burst of shots, and then shot after shot after shot for minutes on end."

Morgan reported that Carl Fisher counted 160 shots fired at one small band of elk. He also stated that 811 elk were killed and many more wounded in the eight day season of 1937. In addition, a sizable number of domestic animals, dogs, sheep, goats, horses and cattle, were killed by those who had never bothered to find out exactly what an elk looked like, or didn't care. For a few, the elk hunt was a boon. An estimated 250,000 dollars poured into the local economy from retail sales and from the rescue of lost and stranded hunters. When the Hoh River flooded half-way into the season, trapped hunting parties had to be rescued by horse and canoe. Word of the deteriorating situation in the Hoh River Valley reached Minnie in the high country. In haste, she packed up and headed off the High Divide into the wet, cold chaos below.

The rest of this story is best told by a *Port Angeles Evening News* reporter. The November 18, 1937 headline read,

WOMAN BRINGS BRINNON MAN TO SAFETY

Even though the hunting season is over the men are still talking about their thrilling experiences on the Hoh. T.B. Balch will forever praise Mrs. Minnie Peterson, who brought him to safety in the wake of the rising river. She is one of the outstanding characters in that region, who with her husband operates a pack train. This business which usually calls for the brawn, brain, courage and stamina of only men is carried on by this woman who tackles the job without flinching. In the face of one of the worst storms in the Hoh district, this wonderful woman went out into the night with a lantern and bells on her horses to bring Balch to safety. Seeing the danger of the approaching freshet at noon, he had waded the rising river, and ran three miles for aid. Perhaps no other packer would have braved the hardships of this night of terror, but Mrs. Peterson faced the weather with her well trained ponies. ...in total darkness she brought T.B. Balch and the elk across the river. It was so dark they could not see the head of the horse before them. Plunging into the river which was now belly-deep--that pony bearing two people crossed the river followed by the two ponies with the meat. The greatest danger in crossing was the fear of logs or snags drifting downstream that would have meant disaster to them all. This was the last of the crossing of the river as daybreak revealed that the river was impassable. Many hunters were marooned... Mrs. Peterson has lived in the Hoh district for many years and has seen many hardships, and too much praise cannot be given this fine woman, who toils in fair and stormy weather for a livelihood that her children may attend school. It is understood that two children are attending Washington State College.

In *Frontier Legacy*, author J.R. Rooney reported the casualties of the 1937 Hoh River Elk War. Two hunters were injured when a former Forest Service employee shot a hole in the gasoline lantern pressure tank in their tent. All three sustained serious burns requiring hospitalization. Another hunter was shot and killed in Owl Creek, while yet another was killed trying to ford the Hoh River in a truck. One unlucky hunter wounded himself in the leg and a white horse was shot while being used to pack out elk meat.

As one might guess, there were ramifications. The USFS and Washington State management of wildlife resources came under increased scrutiny. Supporters of a national park used this fiasco as further argument for their cause and the disaster may very well have expedited the process which led to the formation of the Olympic National Park.

---

* Halfway through the season the state liquor store in Forks ran out of whiskey and the town was dry for several days.

CHAPTER ELEVEN

THE RANGER'S ROCKY ROMANCE

One of Oscar's and Minnie's trusted and loyal friends, Maynard Fields, lived to become a quintessential ranger of the Olympic National Park—a ranger's ranger. In the summer of 1938 he worked as Park summer help, stationed at the lookout on Bogachiel Peak. His very serious girl, Claudia,* a redheaded beauty with a disposition to match her hair color, worked behind the counter at Sol Duc. Caludia had met Maynard in 1934 when she worked at Lake Quinault Lodge and he had a job in the woods across the lake. In the summer of 1936 Claudia got a job at Sol Duc and Maynard was hired by the park service. Immediately, Maynard appealed to park superintendent Preston Macy for a backcountry position at Bogachiel Peak, close to Sol Duc and Claudia. In the letter granting this appeal Mr. Macy made it clear that he was <u>confident</u> Maynard's proximity to his girlfriend would not impact Maynard's job performance as fire lookout. This was most certainly the case; however, it is clear from the tales old timers still tell, that the park got somewhat less than a hundred percent of Maynard's time and energy. The following is excerpted from a letter to the author from Cougar Fields, May 1, 2005:

> *Jack Nattinger tells stories of working and camping near Sol Duc Falls and seeing Dad with his flashlight heading back up to Bogachiel Peak in the middle of the night after hiking down after work to court my mom (16 miles round trip and about 3500 foot elevation difference). All my life I have heard stories of the many times dad made that trip...*

The path back home for Ranger Maynard Fields, often traveled after dark.
Bogachiel Peak on far right - taken from Rock Hollow
Cougar Fields Collection

---

* Claudia later became his wife of 50 years.

By late summer 1938, Maynard was heavily invested in this four year courtship. His legendary hikes to Sol Duc alone equaled several Mt. Everest climbs in elevation gains. The effort paid off though, and Maynard and Claudia were getting along famously in spite of the distance between them; that is, until two local young ladies plopped themselves down at the fountain at Sol Duc and began recounting, for all who cared to listen, their adventures in the mountains.

The more interesting parts of their tale had to do with the two nights they spent at Bogachiel Peak with the very handsome, very hospitable and very fun ranger who lived there. They didn't get far before Claudia, who was behind the counter at the time, had fire in her eyes to match her hair color. Edna Anderson and the home-economics teacher from Forks took the hint and left Sol Duc in haste. By chance, Pete carried the next letter to Maynard. It smoldered in a saddle bag all the way up the mountain and was literally too hot to handle. Maynard used all his skill as a firefighter and more to bring this situation under control. Two and a half years later Claudia is still steaming in this post-script to a letter addressed to Minnie.

Claudia and Maynard at Bogachiel Peak - August 1938
Cougar Fields collection

Minnie brings Claudia for a visit - August 1938
Cougar Fields collection

...we [Dora Byrne and Claudia] will take our sleeping bags and set out for the low divide—If we are good enough hikers maybe we can get over to Sol Duc to see you—we will wear shorts Minnie and stop and see all the rangers like some of the chick-a-dees did the summer I was at Sol Duc. Oh Yeah! Wouldn't Maynard have a fit!

All's well that ends well.
Graves Creek, Quinault - 1939
Cougar Fields collection

Chapter Twelve

Turk to the rescue

Minnie was a keen observer of her outdoor environment, an avid reader* and one who savored her contacts with scientists, many of whom were her clients. So although academic life had not agreed with her, by the time Minnie had reached her thirties she had educated herself on countless subjects. In this process she became acutely aware of how fast the world was changing and that her children would not be making their living from the back of a horse. As each graduated from high school they were sent to Washington State College (now WSU). The Peterson family college tradition began with Vivian in 1935, then Ivan in 1936, Pete in 1941 and Carma in 1945.

Ivan's goal was to study what he loved most, forestry. During the summer he worked for the USFS, the agency with whom he envisioned a future. As a returning senior in 1939, Ivan was anxious to graduate and begin his career. Before heading back to college he received word that the elk exclosure four miles up the Hoh River trail had been damaged by a windfall.

Tagging calves for elk study on the Hoh - June 23, 1937
Left to right - Carl Elling, Ivan Peterson, Harold Mandery, George Ohmert, Milton Moore
Courtesy of U.S. Forest Service

---

*   *National Geographic, and Smithsonian* among other publications.

Ivan and George Ohmert "Turk" hiked up the trail with an axe to fix the problem. Once at the exclosure Ivan climbed the tree they had found leaning into the fence and began to chop. In one awkward instant, Ivan's career as a ranger, three of his toes and the end of his foot were gone. George Ohmert put a tourniquet low on Ivan's leg, ran for the horse corrals at Jackson Ranger Station,* rode back and brought Ivan out on horseback.

That first semester of his senior year Ivan limped noticeably. During the second semester ingenious friends and classmates glued three hacksaw blades inside his shoe for support and promised to whack Ivan if they saw him limping. The limp was cured but Ivan's career plans were finished. The USFS was no longer an option. Minnie was predictably furious. When the dust settled the Forest Service promised to help with more schooling. Subsequently, Ivan was admitted to the WSC School of Veterinary Medicine from which he graduated in 1944.**

Dr. Ivan Peterson with patient - early forties
"They told me it was a small animal clinic."

---

*   Now the Hoh Ranger Station
**   It was Oscar who first calculated that Ivan would "make a fine horse doctor."

CHAPTER THIRTEEN

OSCAR JR. SAVES THE DAY

In the late thirties two ambitious trail building projects were begun above Sol Duc Hot Springs. The first was a reroute of the Deer Lake trail and the second was an extension of the Sol Duc loop trail to Cat Creek Basin and on toward the Bailey Range. The plan included the construction of a trail high on the ridge overlooking the extreme upper end of the Hoh Valley as well as Mount Olympus. Minnie packed the trail crews' camp cross country to Cat Creek Basin. The trail was then built back toward civilization from there as well as farther out toward the Baileys.

Cat Creek Basin had been chosen for its central location and abundance of water. Cooking supplies were dropped in the basin, but dynamite was left on the horses, and then packed out to the bluffs at trails end. Minnie's packers always handled the dynamite very gingerly and winced as they watched the trail crew carelessly pitch the fifty pound boxes of high explosives.

Dynamite, although hard on the nerves, was actually easy to pack in its uniform wood boxes.* Other freight was not as easy. For instance, the 300 pound cook stove had to be stripped and placed high on one side of Minnie's largest horse. The smaller parts were then boxed and put low on the other side. Almost as nerve wracking as dynamite were the cases of eggs on the weekly grocery list. Minnie was always in her best humor when the typical load of forty dozen eggs had been lifted off the horses at the Cat Creek camp. A trail crew could not survive without eggs and for this reason Old Babe, who always carried this most precious cargo, was turned loose of the pack string so she could go at her own pace. The last run to Cat Creek in the month of July 1939 was no exception.

By midday Minnie and Pete had reached Sol Duc Park with two short pack strings and Babe bringing up the rear with the eggs. They stopped to rest just below Heart Lake. Now Minnie always encouraged her horses to roll after they were unpacked. It's a cowboy tradition to value a horse by the number of rolls it will do—usually $50 a roll. Unfortunately, Babe was still very much loaded when she lay down heavily. That really didn't get Minnie and Pete's attention, but what did, was the gentle rocking she started a few minutes later.

Pete remembers very little of this trip but he does remember vividly the terror of this moment and he does remember "sailing" (his words) off his horse and across the meadow with adrenaline fueled strength and speed to the rescue of the eggs. Pete's display of athleticism was due in equal part to Minnie's urgings and Pete's own nightmarish vision of having to present the Cat Creek cook with the primary ingredient for an omelet of monstrous proportions. Minnie was lucky again, the eggs were saved. The men of Cat Creek Camp would have another week of eggs and pancakes for breakfast.

After the 1939 season of packing for the Cat Creek Camp, Minnie figured she had packed about everything you could put on a horse. She found out just how wrong she was early the following summer when she opened her cabin door to a clearly agitated ranger. Ranger Buckmaster needed a little favor. As he explained further, Minnie realized that the favor really wasn't so little after all. The corpse that was laying in the trail just above Sol Duc Falls weighed about 250 pounds. Oscar had warned her there would be days like this.

Years later Minnie recalled two problems she faced in accomplishing the mission. The first was how to protect the body from bruising and the second, how to get "dead weight" on a horse. Minnie took extra tarps, ropes, a blanket and the ranger up the trail with her. They rolled the body in blankets and tarps, boosted it across a riding saddle, tied it securely and headed back down the trail taking special care to avoid pack bumpers.**

---

* As recalled by Minnie to Will Muller in *Western Horseman* December 1975.
** Pack bumpers are limbs, trees, and rocks that protrude into the trail.

CHAPTER FOURTEEN

OSCAR'S SNIDER IN THE THIRTIES AND FORTIES

Ranger Sanford Floe and his wife Esther had three children, Dorothy, Maxine, and Sandy. In this excerpt from a letter to the author, Sandy recalls his early memories of life at Snider Ranger Station:

Snider was also the site of a large CCC* camp during the depression years, so the facilities there were large during those days and for several years thereafter. One of the buildings there was the "shop." The shop was where a large part of the activity at the ranger station took place, at least in the mind of a kid. I had the run of the whole camp so I got to be where the action was. My dad spent a lot of his time in the office. It seemed that he spent almost of all his time there. From my view point he took papers out of one basket, read them, initialed them, and put them in another basket. About as boring a job as someone could have in my eyes. Now Oscar had the best and neatest job in the world! He was always found in the shop or over at the barn. There was always neat activity going on around him no matter where he was. So when it came to following someone around, guess where the "Floe Kid" was? He always greeted me with "Hello there, Sandy!" Real loud and in a neat rhythmic voice. What's neat to a kid is to be recognized and greeted that way...as an adult would be. He was always building or repairing something interesting and important. As it was 38 miles to Port Angeles, most things were fixed right there at Snider. The route over highway 101 was gravel and full of chuck holes so a trip to PA was an all day event which took careful planning. The shop consisted of a large metal lathe, drill press, welding outfit, huge sharpening stone (30 inches in diameter or so), big anvil, a forge about 5 ft. square, overhead chain operated block and tackle, big vice (a hand pincher I found out the hard way) and bull shaft built in the ceiling that operated numerous belt driven machines. To operate the various belt driven machines the operator had to be sure that the machines that weren't being used were disengaged from their belts and the machine to be used was. There was an electrical switch to engage everything. For many years the ranger station was operated by a Pelton wheel which generated electricity for the whole station. Then after the war (WWII) two large diesel engine/generators were installed. The Pelton wheel and electrical controls were sold. All of the animals loved Oscar. It was an event to go to the barn with him as the animals would rush over to him and vie for his attention. Imagine 12 or more animals doing this. I was told to stay on the outside of the fence until the animals were in their stalls so as to not get kicked as sometimes the animals fought each other in jealous fits. Dad said that Oscar trusted every one of the animals. They were all good friends. One day they agreed to accept some mules from the Quilcene Ranger District which could not be packed. These mules were thoroughly spoiled and of bad temperament. Well, Oscar had them doing their job in a very short time. One morning sometime later, dad was sitting in his office when Oscar came in and was covered with blood. His face was a bloody mess with even some teeth missing. He managed to whisper to dad he was "okay now Sandy" and that he was "sorry about being late in getting the pack string going." It seemed that one of the "new" mules was laying in wait for Oscar to let his guard down and kicked him in the face with both feet! Dad said that as near as he could figure, that Oscar laid out on the barn for about three hours before regaining consciousness. The pack string, including the ornery mule, was outside the office door "packed and ready to go to work!" Oscar had to have regained consciousness and then put the string together after being kicked almost beyond recognition. `Course dad said he would have none of that and got Oscar to a doctor. Many times I hear that story and at the end of the narration dad would say, "Oscar was one of the toughest men I ever knew."

---

*   Civilian Conservation Corps

President Roosevelt's entourage arrives at Snider Work Center, September 1937.

Note: Motorcycle escort and Civilian Conservation Corps men at attention in upper right, Oscar's shop - upper middle, Secret Service in fedoras along with assorted politicians and mucky muks.

Photo courtesy of US Forest Service.

CAMP FIRE PERMITS
ISSUED HERE FREE
REPORT FIRES HERE

In the following letter, Oscar gave Sanford a progress report:

Forks, Wash.
Dec. 29, 1940

S.M. Floe
District Ranger
Snider Ranger Station
Port Angeles, Wash.

Dear Sir;
Reference is being made to your letter of Dec.12.

In regards to my injury, I do not wish to close the case, because even though all the dental work has been done, the healing of the injury has not reached a satisfactory termination. That is, there is a very hard lump in my lower lip.

Sincerely,
Oscar A Peterson

UNITED STATES DEPARTMENT OF AGRICULTURE

FOREST SERVICE

NORTH PACIFIC REGION

ADDRESS REPLY TO
REGIONAL FORESTER
AND REFER TO

BOX 4137
POST OFFICE BUILDING
PORTLAND, OREGON

December 21, 1950

Oscar A. Peterson
Forks,
Washington

Dear Mr. Peterson:

When the men who work with the physical aspects of Service employment enter on retirement, they leave behind tangible results of their efforts. This is certainly true in your case. Many a shelter, cabin and bridge stand as evidence that you were on the job, and that your accomplishment was good.

You have been a resourceful leader, successful in inspiring others with your enthusiasm, and one with whom other men like to work. Your reputation of "having a way with stock" is an indication of an understanding nature, and supports the fact that you found in the Service your rightful place by fitting into an organization where good woodsmanship is an essential quality.

May you have all of the joys of retirement, and many years of life in which to spend it.

Very sincerely yours,

H. J. ANDREWS
Regional Forester

97

Stories abound about the camp at Snider, a place full of young men, mostly CCC's and USFS employees. Maxine Floe, Sandford and Esther's younger daughter, was not the wallflower type and never missed an opportunity to show off her skills on horseback. The exhibitions incited dares from the camp population for feats of ever-increasing difficulty. On one occasion this escalated into a dare to jump the camp garbage pit. As usual, Maxine waited until she had a good crowd and backed her horse to get a good run at it. Horse and rider fully anticipated making the jump, until the last second, when the horse changed its mind and slammed on the brakes catapulting Maxine head first into the smelly pit. The good news was the landing was soft; the bad news had to do with unspecified damages to a preteen ego.

Left to right - Maxine and Dorthy Floe at Snider Ranger Station.
Marge Cowan collection

CHAPTER FIFTEEN

FRANCIS FARMER ESCAPES TO SOL DUC

By the first week of September 1941 the Hollywood paparazzi were berserk. The stunningly beautiful young woman that had consumed so many column inches over the past six years had gone missing. The actress they had built up and described as the "screen's most outstanding find of 1936" and who had finished three movies in the previous four months had vanished without a trace.* Having to simply report that she had disappeared was so unsatisfying after years of feeding frenzy. Her rocky marriage, her controversial prose and poetry, her trip to Russia, the film she made with Bing Crosby, and her role as Calamity Jane–with Francis in town life had been good for the gossips.

Editors screamed for the story and imaginative writers supplied them with interesting tales. "Crazy and Irrational Exploits" were reported to fill the lost months. Some said Francis had gone into hiding out of fear of communists, others reported she had hid in her room in an advanced state of paranoia and could not carry on a rational conversation. These were all lies; none was true.

That first Wednesday evening in September 1941 only a handful of people knew where Frances Farmer was. Minnie was one of them. Minnie, Frances, and Dora Byrne, the Sol Duc Ranger's wife, were huddled, cozy up to the fire, at Minnie's high camp on the Sol Duc–Hoh Divide. The contrast between Frances´ life in California and this shared moment in the Olympic high country could not have been starker. Here, there were no phones, no agents, no deadlines, no directors, no blinding headaches, no domineering mother, only camp conversation above the white noise of the Hoh River a mile below, occasionally punctuated by campfire crackle. For the moment she was free.

By all accounts Frances was also definitely game. She had ridden nine hard miles and that evening the weather closed in, promising a wet night. It did rain. Back on the trail the next day, it was obvious fall was coming to the upper Sol Duc Valley. Flowers were on the decline but wildlife remained visibly abundant, feasting on the late season offerings of the alpine meadows. On the trip across the divide and down the Sol Duc via Deer Lake, "the group tallied 28 deer, four bands of elk, and several bear." (*Port Angeles Evening News*, Sept. 13, 1941) Despite the less than ideal weather, the Park Service reported that "Frances thoroughly enjoyed her trip." ** Minnie enjoyed her short time with Francis Farmer as well, attracted by her free spirit, unconventional thinking and poetry.

The big pool with diving tower - Sol Duc

---

* From Frances Farmer biography, *Shadowland*, by William Arnold

** It was unfortunate that this extended lost weekend at Sol Duc that Frances used to refresh herself was later used by her enemies to disparage her and the myth that she was descending into madness during this period prevailed. Over the next ten years she was committed to Western State Hospital and then recommitted and subjected to the most barbaric psychiatric procedures available at the time: insulin shock treatments, electroconvulsive shock therapy, possibly ice baths, and supposedly a trans-orbital lobotomy.

CHAPTER SIXTEEN

WAR REACHES SOL DUC

Life changed suddenly even on the remote Olympic Peninsula with the bombing of Pearl Harbor, evidenced by this letter to Minnie from Oscar on December 9, 1941.

Dear Minnie-

*I can't come home until Saturday after dinner—as we are not allowed on the highway after dark. Turk more than likely will be down with me. They had to send east for that piece for the car so it will be some time before we have the car again. So Minnie dear you be ready to go to the Hoko after the cow in Turk's car. Sunday we will take the horses over the hill, or go to Sol Duc and get our stuff. There are sure plenty of activity on the highway now army trucks all times of night. Dearie we are sure rushing the trees in * we will be through by Christmas I hope. We have a complete black out here at Snider. We will have to get blinds for our house it is hard to tell how long this is going to last. You will be quite surprised to hear from me. How are you getting along with your differing horses. I will close for this time.*

Lovingly yours,
Oscar

With the beginning of WWII came the end of trail building in the western Olympics. The trail crew left to join the army and in early summer 1942, Minnie packed the last vestiges of the Cat Creek Camp back to Sol Duc.

With part of his foot gone and having less than perfect balance, the army had no interest in Ivan. He spent his summers interning at a vet practice in Los Angeles. Pete, however, was drafted soon after he returned from college in 1942 as were Minnie's other packing helpers.** When Micky Merchant had the time he helped, but for most of the war years Minnie was on her own.

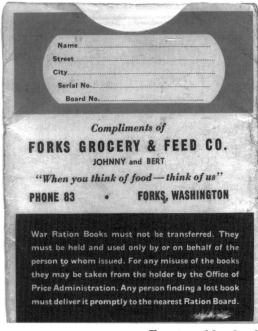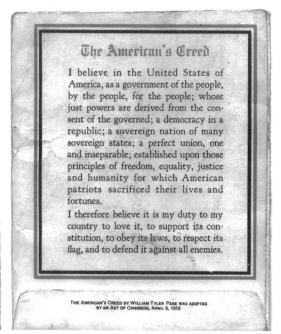

Front and back of WWII ration books.

---

* Planting trees
** Oscar Jr. (Pete) recalls that everyone in boot camp complained unnecessarily about the drill instructor. The fact that Oscar had no complaints and actually thought he was a nice guy speaks volumes about the way Minnie ran her home and business.

Micky spent long winters in California, Arizona, and Mexico. He prospected and worked as a ranch hand. No matter what happened, he always knew he had friends up north. In a letter postmarked January 19, 1942 from Yuma Arizona, Micky writes,

"Deal us in."
Micky in Yuma - undated.

This is kind of a hard luck story. I had a gun stuck in my back the other night and I reached right up for the stars without a word. I was over to Winterhaven, Calif. that eve and done a little gambling. Cashing in a little I guess there, fellows saw and followed me and played take all. And they did. If either one of you could see your way clear to let me have 5 or 10 please send it soon…I hope you will write soon, cash or no cash. I am real well and hope you folks are all well.

I am, as ever,
Mick

In 1942 Minnie packed building materials for the Pyramid Peak air defense lookout above Lake Crescent and continued to supply Bogachiel Peak whose main function had switched from spotting fires to spotting planes. Air defense was not a seasonal activity so Minnie moved supplies to the peak as early as the snow pack allowed. Kitchen, heat and light were all powered by ninety pound propane tanks that Minnie could just get on a horse. The work was hard but steady and the pay checks all cashed.

While Minnie made her contribution to the war effort supplying the high country fire lookouts turned air patrol stations, Sol Duc was abuzz with rumors of what would be its contribution to the allied war machine. U-boats and surface ships were hammering allied shipping and the Generals and Admirals were not happy.

Howard Hughes had the answer. He proposed building a monster flying machine capable of carrying huge amounts of troops and cargo. Hughes's entire project was plagued by the fact that it was somewhat ahead of the technology curve.* One of the numerous engineering problems had to do with the strength and weight of building materials. Although the prescribed solution was wood, not just any tree would do. Eventually the engineers' search narrowed to the privately held 160 acres that surrounded the Sol Duc Hot Springs Resort. This timber was owned by the logging company, Burrowes and Fox. Before the timber could be harvested, Burrowes and Fox's right as an inholder to cut timber had to be affirmed by the Supreme Court. By late fall 1942 logging operations began.

Oscar and the infamous camp dog, Spike.

Barnyard at Sol Duc turned logging camp - 1942.

---

*   It was two decades later before a plane of similar dimensions became practical.

The toys that the big kids play with. - Stan Burrowes

Stan Burrowes remembers:

I will speculate that Dave was showing Oscar one of the "toys that the big kids play with " and telling Oscar how utilitarian this machine was around his Sequim ranch in the winter when logging was shut down due to weather.

I know first hand that when Oscar and Minnie were at the Springs at the same time Dave and Louise were there, they got together for a good stiff drink before dinner and a long and congenial dinner in the camp cook house. Reminiscence of Minnie and Louise' younger days in the West End and world affairs in general were part of that dinner conversation. All four were well read and well informed on current affairs and if you were going to engage in their conversation, you better have done your homework. Minnie, who I had more contact with than Oscar, had a keen mind and the ability to deliver what was on her mind with clarity and as few words as possible. Small wonder why she and her packing business was so popular.

Oscar, Dave Burrowes and Spike - 1943

Compared to other timber camps, Sol Duc was a Shangri-La for loggers. Burrowes and Fox put their men up in the resort cabins, set up a cook house and hired a chef of exceptional talent. Louise Burrowes, Dave Burrowes' wife, did her part as well. On hot days she made a routine trip to La Poel on Lake Crescent and never failed to bring back a couple of cases for the men just in time for them to enjoy a cold brew after work.*

Although Minnie was sad to see the timber go below the Hot Springs, having the Burrowes and Fox headquarters set up within sight of her cabin did present certain financial possibilities which she quickly capitalized on. Sixty years later Stan Burrowes, college student at the time and son of Dave, claimed that by way of the card table Minnie acquired a considerable share of the resources Howard Hughes was sending to the Sol Duc Camp. Furthermore, when pressed, Stan seemed very certain that in the summer of 1943 Minnie's revenue stream from games of chance must have exceeded her revenue from all other sources. Minnie's mantra was predictably "wasn't I lucky?"** In his notes Stan Burrowes remembers the unanimous sentiments of those who worked in the big timber at Sol Duc, "It was the best job with the best working conditions of their lives." It didn't seem to matter that they lost a few dollars to Minnie.

---

* From Stan Burrowes´notes.
** It was her self-depreciating way to explain her consistent winning. She would never say "aren't I good?"

Oscar Jr. (Pete) - 1945
"Somewhere in Europe"

Within a month of VE Day the GI´s had begun to stream back from the European theatre on their way to Japan. Pete was among them. He headed straight for Sol Duc where tourist season was in full swing and the celebrating hadn't stopped.* At the same time Wilma Gilbert, her sister and brother-in-law were doing their own celebrating. After quitting their Boeing jobs and before returning home to the Midwest, they decided to treat themselves first to a week at Sol Duc.

Wilma was quite taken by the looks of the blond soldier she had seen riding out of the woods next to the lady with the breeches and enormous hat. Although she noticed him again at the Sol Duc store and dance hall, they never spoke. Wilma did leave her address with the woman behind the counter at Sol Duc. Big sister Roberta could not believe her sister could be so forward. "Furthermore, hadn't Wilma seen his mother? They were obviously hillbillies."

Back home in Arkansas Roberta was quick to fill her mom in on what kind of character Wilma was writing to out west. To confirm her suspicions and get this long distance affair over, Mrs. Gilbert wrote the Forks town Marshall a letter of inquiry regarding person and family of one Oscar C. Peterson (Pete). Fortunately for Wilma and Pete the letter that came back contained a rave review assuring Mrs. Gilbert that the Petersons were "upstanding, prosperous, the cream of the crop, and pillars of Forks society". Marshall Hunley's letter went on and on. Working in Wilma and Pete's favor at this time was the fact that Mrs. Gilbert did not read this letter of recommendation with the prior knowledge that the marshal was a favorite drinking buddy of Oscar Sr. Shortly thereafter on April 23, 1946 in Arkansas, Oscar Jr. and Wilma May Gilbert were married.

Home with mom in the mountains - 1945.

---

*   Pete spent the first month after the war in Pilzen, Czechoslovakia , then traveled across Europe in a 40 and 8 box car (40 men or 8 horses) to Le Harve, France where they shipped out to New York.

From the beginning, Sol Duc Hot Springs had been a meeting place where cupid's arrows were often thick. The rhapsody of the river and spectacular mountain scenery set the stage. The amenities at Sol Duc also contributed to the romantic setting. In addition to the pools, there was the dance hall with Percy on the accordion, miniature golf, horseback riding and tennis. There was also the Lovers Lane Trail with its terminus near beautiful Sol Duc Falls. With all these advantages the little guy with the bow and arrows still needed occasional help, and Minnie was always there to oblige. Letters from the smitten tell the stories.

Oriskany, N.Y.
Oct. 20, 1954

Dear Minnie,

Just wanted to assure you once again, of my most sincere thanks for your kind hospitality extended Mary and I, by both you and Oscar. Also the courteous and efficient manner in which you handled our trips in the mountains. It was the nicest trip that I've ever had. For that reason, I feel that I should like for you to share with me a secret.

I returned home night before last to an empty house where I have lived alone every since the death of my mother. I've never been married for some reason or other and as I unlocked the door, I have never felt so lonely in all my life. I shall miss the pleasant friendliness of both you and Oscar, but above all I miss Mary. I am not ashamed to admit that I loved the girl. I have urged her to get away from the Springs and when she gets her affairs cleaned up to let me know and I'll come back and get her. My job is such that I think I can give her most anything she wants. And we can always come back from time to to time and see both you and Oscar. I'd appreciate it if you would go down there and make sure that she is aright. I am sending you within a day or two, a little present. I hope you like it, and as soon as I have some pictures I'll see to it that you get some that I think you'll like.

Wishing both you and Oscar nothing but the best, I remain as ever,
K. Worden

Hoquiam, Wash.
July, 4, 1958

Dear Minnie,

How are you? I am fine. I haven't got the pictures developed yet!
I was wondering if you would do me a favor! You know where you register for a cabin well I wondered if you would see who was renting cabin 61 for the week of the 4th or as long as they rented it and get their last name and their address and where they live for me. You see I like one of the boys that stayed in that cabin. You know how it is when you don't know very much about him. I met him in the little pool Monday night. I know his first name but that is all.
Well bye for now and write soon.

Love,
Joan Priebe

P.S. Could you send the information soon? If you can get it.
Thank you!

UNITED STATES
DEPARTMENT OF THE INTERIOR
National Park Service

- - oOo - -

OLYMPIC NATIONAL PARK

Mrs. Oscar Peterson
Sol Duc Hot Springs Base
Port Angeles, Washington

- - oOo - -

Schedule of Basic Rates for the 1947 Season

- - oOo - -

Saddle Horse Service.

    Saddle Horse:
        Per hour $ 1.50
        Per half day   4.00
        Per day   7.00
        Per week   30.00

    Pack and Saddle Horse Service:
        One horse per day $ 6.00
        Two horses per day   5.00 each ← 6
        Three horses per day   5.00 each 5.
        Four or more horses per day   4.00 each ← 5
        Packer per day including packer's saddle horse 10.00

5 or more horses 4 per day per person

Horses fully equipped----nothing else furnished 10% reduction on all
trips seven days or longer.

                        Approved: June 26, 1947.

                        Hillory A. Tolson

                        Hillory A. Tolson,
                        Acting Director.

                                                    1168

Minnie's rate schedule

CHAPTER SEVENTEEN

The first post-war year marked the beginning of a parade of helpers and ranch hands that extended well into the 1980's. Since Minnie paid notoriously low wages, the help came, stayed on and became life long friends for other reasons. Some liked the horses, others the woods, some the freedom. Some were relatives, nieces, nephews, grandkids, and great-grandkids. Others had parents who had worked for Minnie. Some were runaways; others had been kicked out of their own homes. Still others were difficult teenagers whose parents had heard of Minnie. Some were adults looking for adventure.

Evelyn Estes, one of the latter, and a horsewoman, was a free spirit who rode her mount from her home in Tennessee and wound up at Sol Duc. Evelyn assisted Minnie in late 1944 and wrote Minnie regularly into the eighties often expressing her admiration and awe.

One of my life's greatest disappointments was not being able to follow you every step into the great outdoors. I kept getting tangled up with that wide yellow stripe down my back—I didn't really know I was such a complete coward till I got into those overpowering Olympics.

In the late forties and early fifties, Martel Gilbert, a high school student and Wilma's youngest brother, worked for Minnie. Martel was thirteen years old in 1948. That year he decided that buying a bus ticket to travel back and forth from Arkansas was a waste of money so from then on he hitch-hiked across the country every summer. In the early 1950's George Brown, a teenager from Enumclaw, worked for Minnie. Later, both George and Martel sent their sons to the Hoh to be under her tutelage.

Rte. 2 Box 369
Olympia, Wash.
Oct 10, 1949

Dear Mrs. Peterson,

I saw your story, written by Erle Howell, in the Magazine Section of the Seattle Sunday Times. I am interested in becoming a guide in Alaska or the Olympics but as yet I am not old enough and have not got the experience. I am 15 years old and have got to go to high school three more years but I was wondering if there wasn't something I could do to help you during my summer vacations.

I love the woods and am in them as much as possible. Every Friday evening after school I cut enough wood to last the weekend at home and then I start for the Black Hills with my two dogs and don't come back until Sunday evening.

I don't know much about guiding but I could learn fast. I wouldn't expect to get paid. All I am interested in is the experience I need. If there is anything I can do to help you please answer. I don't (over) care what it is. I have been to the Sol Duc Hot Springs before and I am sorry I didn't see you there.

Sincerely

George Brown
Rte. 2 Box 369
Olympia, Washington

P.S.
Enclosed is a picture of one of my dogs and me.

George and his faithful friend.

Another devoted helper in the late fifties and early sixties was Ann St. John, Minnie's barefoot beatnik assistant. These were the years rumors flew and speculations proliferated after word got out that a dam was being planned for the Oxbow.* Its reservoir would extend to the park boundary and cover all but a few of the 300 acres of Minnie's land on the Hoh, land that Minnie had put thirty years of her life into. It would cover thousands of acres of bottom land and winter range for the valley's elk herds. It would flood hundreds of miles of trout and salmon spawning streams.

Both Minnie and Ann celebrated when the final feasibility study was published and the conclusion was negative. The geology of the Oxbow would not support a dam. Ann was last heard from living on Waldron Island, a paradise for a minimalist—no power, phones or daily mail service. She faithfully wrote Minnie over the years ending every letter with a zinger of some sort. A 1961 Christmas card ends with "What do you think of anarchy as a form of government and philosophy, I think it might solve everything". An April 20, 1968 letter ends with "Take good care of your chess men and prepare them for battle!"

Mrs. Oscar Peterson 12-18-58

THE FARTHEST WEST NEWSPAPER IN THE UNITED STATES

FORKS

VOLUME XXIX — FORKS FORUM, FORKS, WASH.

Hoh Bow Hydro-Electric and Recreation Development Project Approved For Investigation By Washington Public Power Supply System

A hydro-electric and recreation development project on the Hoh River in Jefferson County was approved for active investigation by the Washington Public Power Supply System at a quarterly meeting of the Board of Directors in Seattle last week.

The action by the WPPSS to file for a Federal Power Commission preliminary permit was recommended in resolutions recently adopted by the Commissioners of the Clallam and Jefferson County Public Utility Districts. The Clallam PUD resolution requested the WPPSS to "undertake investigations and all steps necessary to determine the physical and financial feasibility of constructing a hydro-electric project of maximum capabilities at the Oxbow site on a schedule best adapted to the power needs of its members and consistent with the needs of the Olympic Peninsula for power generation and transmission facilities."

The resolution also urged the WPPSS to "plan and carry out the development of the project in a manner which will result in the maximum use of the reservoir and adjoining lands for recreation purposes and cooperate with all interested agencies in preserving and expanding the fish and game resources of the river and reservoir."

The District pledged its cooperation and agreed to transfer its present water rights on the Hoh River as well as property it owns at the Oxbow site under mutually satisfactory terms if the project is proven feasible.

The Jefferson County PUD Commissioners in a joint meeting with the Commissioners of Clallam County on November 19 endorsed the action taken by the Clallam County PUD.

Art Reynolds, President of the Clallam County PUD, stated, "The proposed project will result in the creation of a new recreation resource of great value to Clallam County and particularly the Forks area in addition to providing a much needed power supply at a point on the system now dependent on remote power sources."

T. H. Baker, Jefferson County PUD Commissioner, said, "The project should be a real stimulus and asset in the future development and use of the timber and other resources of western Jefferson County. Action by the WPPSS is timely and will benefit the entire Olympic Peninsula."

"The Hoh River project has long been recognized for its power potential and the investigations now being undertaken by the WPPSS should result in the ultimate development of a sound and adequate power supply for the area which would include the maximum use of all feasible hydro-electric sites supplemented with thermal plants as needed," Grover C. Greimes, Clallam County PUD Commissioner and President of the WPPSS, stated.

Location Being Considered - - -

The project now being considered would be located near the intersection of the Hoh River with U. S. Highway 101, approximately 12 miles south of the Town of Forks.

A dam 200 feet in height would create a lake of approximately 4,000 acres and back water up to the boundary of the Olympic National Park. The plant would have an installed capacity of 60,000 kilowatts and would be integrated with the Bonneville system by transmission lines extended from Port Angeles. The location of the project near a large bow in the river caused the WPPSS to designate it as the "Hoh Bow Hydro-Electric and Recreation development Project".

In order to provide a power supply for western Clallam County and to replace inadequate and costly power from a diesel plant a small diversion project at the Oxbow site was investigated and designed by the Clallam County PUD in 1953. Availability of BPA power at Port Angeles and the construction of a 69 kv transmission line by the PUD from Port Angeles to Forks caused the PUD to drop plans for the smaller hydro plant.

"The hydrology of the Hoh River with the heaviest rainfall in the state and glacier and snow melt make this stream one of the best in the state for power production," Owen W. Hurd, Managing Director of WPPSS stated.

The WPPSS is a joint operating agency organized by 13 Public Utility Districts to provide a future power supply for its members. Other projects now under active investigation by the WPPSS are the Ben Franklin Dam on Columbia River and the Packwood Lake project in Lewis County.

---

* The Hoh Oxbow; a U-turn in the Hoh River

Seek Hoh permit

WASHINGTON (AP) — Washington Public Power Supply System, Kennewick, Wash., Wednesday asked the Power Commission for a preliminary permit for a proposed hydroelectric project on the Hoh River in Jefferson County, Wash.

The project would be located near Forks. It would include a dam 120 feet high and a power house to contain two 33,500-horse-power turbines with 26,500 kilowatt generators.

The system is a municipal corporation under Washington law, composed of 13 member public utility districts. The power to be generated would meet growing requirements of the district, with any surplus to be delivered into the Northwest Power Pool.

A preliminary permit does not authorize any construction. It gives the holder priority while making the studies necessary to prepare any application for a commission license.

5209 NE 88th Street
Vancouver, Washington
May 16, 1959

Mrs. Peterson
Forks, Washington

Dear Mrs. Peterson:

I would like a job working in the mountains this summer. I will graduate from high school on June Irst of this year and am enrolled at Washington State College for the fall semester.

I have a horse of my own which I could bring with me if you could use me working with horses. She is an 8 year old Colorado quarter mare and I have had her for six years.

My mother is a registered nurse and works at the Veterans Hospital in Vancouver. My father is a carpenter and farmer. We have lived on farms in Colorado and Missouri.

I will be I8 in August and am 5'3½" and weigh II5 lbs. I do not smoke or drink.

Your consideration will be greatly appreciated.

I know Mrs. Betty Lenoir who lives on Crescent Lake.

Sincerely yours,

Ann St. John

Letter of inquiry from Ann St. John

"How about a couple hands of poker?"
Minnie, Ann St. John, and Ellery Miles - 1959

CHAPTER EIGHTEEN

A NEW BEGINNING

In 1962 Wayne Kirk, the son of noted nature writer Ruth Kirk and Park Ranger Louis Kirk, came to work for Minnie. As far as Minnie was concerned, Wayne came to the job eminently qualified. He knew how to work and just as importantly, he could give Minnie a real run for her money in the game of chess. In the end however, much more was required of Wayne. At eighteen he was present during the saddest period of Minnie's life, the passing of her husband Oscar. In addition to the emotional support he provided, Oscar had been the one who shoed the horses, trucked them, made sure the winter feed was put up, kept the tack in shape, bought supplies for her trips and did the driving for her.*

Minnie was visibly weakened by the loss and this was unnerving for the family. Few had ever seen her shed a tear. Oscar Jr. (Pete) took some time off work and with Wayne's help, finished Minnie's packing contracts for the summer of 1962. In the fall, every effort was made to convince Minnie that the "62" season should be her last: "How could you, without Oscar? You're 65 years old. You've worked hard; it's time to slow down. You know how that knee has been bothering you. Your farm will keep you plenty busy." The refrain was repeated by caring friends and relatives.

These sentiments were no consolation to Minnie. She was not about to give up both her true loves in one summer. She began plotting her escape from civilization, this time a final and permanent escape. In the spring of 1963 Minnie moved to a secluded cabin in the Rainforest. From her headquarters there she continued to guide for another sixteen years.

Minnie and Oscar clearing land on Hoh River Ranch - 1960.

---

* All of Minnie's attempts at learning to drive ended badly. In her last try she tested the structural integrity of their pick-up on a stump.

THE AFTERWARD

My introduction to Minnie came through the pictorial section of the Seattle Times newspaper. This was very early spring of 1949. I was a 14 year old boy living in the hills outside Littlerock, Washington and, for me, just thinking about the possibility of working up in the Olympics was beyond my wildest dreams. I was a real shy kid, but somehow I managed to write a letter and sent it off to Minnie Peterson, Pack and Saddle Horses, Forks, Washington. I didn't know her actual address but hoped my letter would somehow find its way. I waited and dreamed, but summer arrived and I didn't get a response. Needless to say, my dreams were dashed. But at Christmas I got a card from Minnie telling me if I was still interested I could come up the following summer. There's no way of explaining what that meant to me, my mind wasn't on much else, and time went so slow before school let out. My parents drove me up to Forks, got to meet Minnie and Oscar and then left me for three months. That was my first time away from home, but I liked Minnie right away and was really looking forward to a dream fulfilled. I'm probably not very objective about what kind of person she was, as the rose-colored glasses I was wearing made everything seem beautiful. I only remember her as one of the most kind, caring, joyous and wonderful people I have ever known. I think I worshipped her, and she was a significant influence on my life. She's not the kind of person you could ever forget, and I can still hear her laugh as she played a trick on me or someone else, or stumped us with one of the puzzles she always had in her purse.

In those days, Minnie and Oscar lived on the ranch in Forks. The first thing we did after I arrived was go up to where Minnie's family had homesteaded on the Hoko River to get the horses to be used for the pack season. Minnie had been born and raised there, but there were still no roads into the ranch. The horses ran most of the year there on open range. There was only one we could catch, but the others followed it back to the barn, and we were able to get halters on all of them. Then we took them down the railroad tracks to the road where we could truck them to Forks. Then came the process of shoeing, and that was a real rodeo. It seems to me Oscar and someone else did the majority of that work, and it was work! Those horses seemed mostly wild to me, and some of them had to have a foot tied up for a while before you could put a shoe on it. They jumped and snorted, and fell, but eventually they gave up. (I later thought about that when people would let their kids run behind and underneath the horses, like they were on a merry-go-round, but the horses never hurt anyone.) After the stock was ready to go to work, we trucked them down to where the Hoh road takes off from the highway, and then rode them up to the ranch—to get them broken in. Saw black bears along the road that you don't normally get to see when driving.

1950 was the year the upper Hoh Bridge was out.* They were in the process of replacing it, but we could not take the horses across, so our trips up the Hoh consisted of packing people in from the ranger station to the guard station, and then up to the bridge. There was an accident that summer. The work crew was pulling a stringer across when the snag the winch was anchored to broke off and knocked one of the crew members onto the ledge they had blasted out for the end of the stringer. If he had stayed still he would have been okay, but he rolled over and fell 140 feet into the river. The whole river has to squeeze through that narrow gorge and it was really moving. They found him three days later under a log jam quite a ways down river. We were camped at the guard station when they brought him out in a body bag on the back of a mule.

We set up camp a ways below the ranger station, and that's where people would meet us for the trip up the river. Minnie and Oscar had just bought a pair of matched white mules. They were beautiful, but not entirely broke. I learned one thing interesting about mules. With a horse that is prone to kicking, you can tie a tire to a foot and it will kick and kick until it learns not to do that. Well, we tied a tire to one of the mule's feet and it didn't kick it at all. We figured a mule was really smart to learn that quickly, and after a while removed the tire. The next time I walked behind the mule it kicked me right in the chest. It was smart all right, smart enough to know the difference between kicking a tire and kicking a person. On one of our trips up the Hoh, Minnie was taking the Margaret McKenney party in. Ms. McKenney was quite a naturalist, was a past president of the state Audubon Society, and by this time seemed to me to be quite an elderly lady. She and one of her male companions wanted to ride those pretty white mules. Minnie tried to talk them out of it, but they insisted. Minnie had a way of letting people learn from their mistakes so she just backed off, but she did get up earlier than usual the next morning and took each mule off in the trees to try to get the buck out of them and she did manage to convince Ms. McKenney to let me lead her mule. The gentleman was determined that he was a good enough horseman to ride on his own. It was a slow trip, as Ms. McKenney had me stop frequently and help her off so she could take little side

---

* The modern name for the bridge is High Hoh Bridge.

trips off the trail to study the fungi that grew at different elevations. I had been told a lot more than I ever wanted to know about fungi, and I think Minnie was getting pretty irritated with the slow pace. But then we got some action. The gentleman on the other mule had been riding at the back of the string and maybe the mule was getting tired of the pace also, because it took off with him. I heard some yelling and here he came passing everything else on the trail. He shot past me but I couldn't try grabbing him for fear of losing old Ms. McKenney. Up ahead we found him, unhurt but dumped off. He was at the spot before you get to the guard station where the trail winds in and out above the river through all those ravines. Apparently the mule took one of those bends too fast for the rider, and we had to pull him back up to the trail. I looked at Minnie's face and could tell she was having a hard time to keep from laughing. I think she did a lot of laughing inside.

For a while at the guard station the deer were so friendly they came and stood around camp. Minnie said it was because they were less afraid of us than the cougars. The next day as we were headed back down river, the cougar tracks were so heavy in some places they had padded down the dirt that the horse had kicked up the day before. Those were pretty easy, relaxing rides. We'd take a party in one day, camp that night then come back out the next day. Minnie said the river was too milky to be good fishing, but she knew where to find big trout in the small streams that ran to the river. On one of those trips, when we returned to our camp below the ranger station, a bear had come through, went through one side of our tent and out the other without bothering anything inside. The tent must have just been in his way.

I'm not sure how Minnie was with other people, especially other kids that worked with her, and I know there were a lot who did. But I don't remember her ever being angry with me. At least she didn't show it. She got a pretty stern look on her face once in a while, like the time I lost a string of horses in the dense rainforest. She was leading a string of a couple of horses and the two mules tied on in back. I was following with another four horses. Minnie had told me not to ride too close to those mules because they might kick my horse. It was a nice warm day, and I think I was pretty drowsy. The next thing I knew I heard a crack, and it was the sound of a mule hoof against my horse's nose. I hadn't been paying attention and got too close. My horse reared back, it spooked the string and they took off running through the jungle. It took half a day to find the horses and get all the packs and gear back together. One of the horses had caught his lead rope on a tree and wound it around it until it had snubbed its nose right down to the ground. I don't remember Minnie saying a thing. I was very embarrassed and had learned a lesson. Maybe she knew that. I think she read people especially well.

I didn't know Oscar as well as Minnie. I only saw him when we were at Forks, and then he came home only on week ends. He was working at the time at the Snider Ranger Station. The three

of us would pick blackberries, check out tack up on the Hoh or at the little cabin at Sol Duc, go visiting, or just fool around. The timing was pretty bad for regular packing. Not only was the Hoh bridge out, but so was the one at Sol Duc, so we didn't pack any at all there. When we had breaks in between pack trips I built fence at the Hoh ranch, much of it along the road. Most of the time we were at Forks and there was always plenty for me to do there. They had me milking a cow, but it wasn't a dairy cow, it was a Hereford. And it didn't like being milked—had to use kicking chains on it all the time. I don't know who had to milk it when I wasn't there. Maybe Martel. I think he was Wilma's nephew, and was visiting Pete and Wilma that summer. Martell and I spent quite a bit of our spare time together –went riding a lot, and would sometimes ride into town, tie the horses, and go to the movie. Just like in the westerns. Martell was a more aggressive rider than me. He was riding a little grey horse called Mousie. She had a bad habit of taking the bit and running off with him, but he would stay with her, even jumping fences and when she got tired of running he would push her until she was about ready to drop. The horse I rode most of the time was Flossie. She had some bad habits too. For one thing, she didn't like to be caught. Most of the time that I would go to catch her she would take off running to the other end of the field. When I followed her up there, she would run back to the other end. But when I started to that end, she would come running toward me, lay back her ears, and turn around kicking. But then she would stop and let me catch her. She was just bluffing I guess. I also had to be a little careful mounting her, to make sure she didn't nip me in the back or kick me in the front. But I enjoyed riding her once I got on. I had worked around animals a lot, but was a real greenhorn when it came to riding. (I wondered years later whether Minnie gave me that horse because it was the easiest of the bunch to work with, or whether it was to toughen me up. I wish I had asked about that when I had a chance) They had recently logged the hill behind the barn, Flossie and I could almost find our way through all that maze up to the top As I recall, Minnie's favorite horse to ride at that time was a buckskin named Vivian, probably named after her daughter. Vivian and Harley had a stallion that they entered in a horse show in Port Angeles. I remember going up there to see it but don't remember how it did. Minnie had a big billy goat in those days and we tied it along the driveway to eat down the grass. The living part of the house was the kitchen. I don't remember the living room ever being used. It wasn't kept heated and reminded me of a museum. There were lots of mounted animals, hides, collections of newspapers and magazines, and I don't know what all. It was just full of interesting stuff. That summer Pete decided to build a new barn. I got the job of hauling and peeling the trees, only I made the mistake of thinking it would be easier for the horse I was using to pull the trees already peeled. What I hadn't figured on is that a peeled tree goes down hill faster than a horse, so it was pretty exciting getting those first few trees out. I peeled the rest of them after I pulled them out. I used a slip to smooth the ground where the barn was going to be built. Those were good days even though I didn't get to do as much packing as I had expected.

In later years I learned more about Minnie's sense of humor. I would take my wife up to visit her, and there was always something funny to remember. One time we saw her after a trip to Oregon where we had learned quite a bit about Llamas. I thought Minnie might be interested, as I was sure she had never had any exposure to this kind of critter. She was her normal polite self and did not interrupt as I told her everything I knew. When I finally ran down, she asked me if I was through. I knew right then I had made a big mistake and sure enough we found out she knew a lot more than we did. One time Grace took some of our friends up to meet Minnie. They were quite elderly, older than Minnie, and really grand ladies themselves. They were so impressed! She was the kind of person you could introduce to royalty and be proud of her. After Oscar was gone and Minnie moved up on the Hoh, it was pretty hard to find a place to sit when you visited. Most of the available space was occupied by magazines and newspapers and other important stuff. So we just cleared a place. Several times we sat around the table for a long time before we realized there was a dog underneath. And one thing I noticed is that Minnie ate the same kind of food she packed-most everything canned. One time after having lunch at the new house that the family had built for Minnie Grace suggested I pick up a little bottle that was lying on the floor by the refrigerator. Minnie came back in the room about that time and said "No, don't move that. I'm using it for an anchor for the mouse trap."

Minnie was one grand lady. I think someone told me one time that she had a lot of kids come to work for her over the years, some of them pretty troubled. If any of them learned half as much from Minnie as I did, about animals, horses, and life in general, then it was well worth their time. I never heard of anyone that didn't love her once they got to know her, and she will always hold a very special place in my heart.

AUTHOR'S REFLECTIONS

(1) Horses

At one time or another every relative, friend and employee wondered whether Minnie really liked people at all. Was it the company or the cards? Did she really like her clients or were they merely the means to an end? Those who knew her were never really sure. What everyone was certain about were Minnie's priorities, and in the back country, at the top of the list, were the horses.

She understood their psychology, sociology, as well as their physiology. Friends were kept together, enemies apart. The old were given lighter loads; the high strung were given space. Minnie knew the habits of all and the limits of all. She was as impatient as the horses to get their loads off at camp. They were checked out, watered, and fed before the word dinner was spoken. Horses were tethered, tied, or let loose for the evening. If a horse was freed, its buddy was tied. At about four in the morning Minnie caught the loose horse and freed its buddy.

Each horse had a different story. Some Minnie purchased, others were trades, and still others were won in card games. More than one was given to Minnie as a lost cause. In Minnie's string there were saints and sinners and all manner in between. It always seemed that as a group, they leaned a little more toward the outlaw side, like Joker, rather than the saint side, like Ranger.

On the whole they were a rough looking lot, but looks didn't count for much. Could the pony carry a load, could the animal keep its head when besieged by yellow jackets or when it smelled the scent of cougar? Would it plunge into a swollen mountain stream on command? Would it walk the planks of the High Hoh Bridge with a boiling torrent 150 feet below? Could it keep its head and feet on a high angle snowfield, shale slope or airy rock ledge? Could it tolerate the temperature extremes of the High Divide and the wet of the Rainforest? As was the case with her employees, Minnie put up with a few quirks if the right proportions of stamina and nerve were present in a horse. Sandy Patton, Minnie's helper in the sixties and seventies, recalls:

Whenever we (packers) started complaining about a horse's bad habits Minnie would point out their good features. Every horse has their good points and their bad points, once you know their bad points you can work around them. If there were further complaints Minnie was also known to comment that packers were easier to replace than pack horses. This gently put me in my place.

The most memorable horses from Minnie's string were: Ranger, Duke, Tiny, Pinky, Buster, Joker, Sparky, Red, Mousey, Ila, Gloria, Hoko, Babe, Besse, Tanis, Blackie, Freddie, Robin, Mandy, Nancy, Hyak, Cindy as well as lead horses Bosco, Bay Bill, Skipper, Vivian and Rats.

(2) The Forks Creamery - 1920

Work at the Forks creamery was generally routine and mundane. Every day was like the last. Cans of cream came from homesteads in and around the town. Most of the cream arrived on wagons or trucks or even in cars. Some was delivered on horseback from the more remote areas around Forks. The homesteaders milked their cows, separated the cream for market, then fed the skimmed milk to calves, pigs, or young elk. This routine was common for folks living on the Hoh. Trips to town from this remote location did not occur every day so how to keep the cream good until it could be transported was a problem.

One settler's solution was a wonderfully cool spring that bubbled out of the ground on his property. The cans were placed right in the water and the cream kept nicely.

The little dairy thrived, that is until one day when the farmer carelessly failed to secure a lid tightly to the top of one of his cream cans. Ordinarily, this would not have been a problem. A few leaves, needles or even insects could be screened out at the creamery without repercussion. In this particular case however, there were repercussions. The problem was bigger and had an eye-watering odor. A civic cat (read skunk) that had been helping himself to the cream had fallen into the open mouth of the can and drowned.

(3) Take care in small towns.

Shortly after retiring from the USFS, Oscar was stopped on Highway 101 south of Forks. The delay was due to road construction and the wait proved to be considerable. While patiently passing the time in his pickup truck, a tourist (Herman Munch) stepped up to the driver's side window wanting to talk. Herman asked Oscar where he was from and when he answered, "Forks," Herman asked if Oscar knew Minnie Peterson. Oscar replied that he reckoned he did. Herman wanted to know if she was a good packer and then asked about her age to which Oscar answered, "Yes," and "about fifty, give or take." It was at this point in the conversation that Herman erred in a way no small town citizen would. He continued his probing by telling Oscar that he was a friend of a soon-to-be-client of Minnie's and had heard from this person that, although Minnie was a real worker, Minnie's husband was kind of a bum who refused to get a job and who let Minnie support him. Herman then enlarged the hole he was digging for himself to the perfect dimension by asking Oscar if he knew Minnie's husband.

(4) Little House on the Prairie—Not!

There were some exceptions to the "Little House on the Prairie" lifestyle of West End pioneers. One unhappy young wife on the Bogachiel River sentenced her husband to the woodshed for life, after an especially monstrous row. He was banned from the house, although she did continue to do his laundry and bring him two meals a day. His contribution to the arrangement included providing her firewood with the caveat that he would not, under any circumstances, stockpile more than one week's wood in advance. The thought that, in the event of his death, a new husband would reap the benefits of his labor was too much for this settler to bear.

(5) Property

From the late twenties to the mid-forties, a time when many families lost their property to back taxes, Minnie acquired over 400 acres of property in Jefferson and Clallam Counties. Most, if not all the land acquisition, was done over Oscar's objections; he feared the tax burden during hard times. Frequently Minnie was able to make land deals in which very little money changed hands. This was due, in part, to the fact that in the old days timber companies placed little value on land that had been cut over. Minnie took the longer view and had the liquidity to back it up. To obtain a "right of way," Minnie paid a neighbor's taxes. Later, in exchange for eighty acres, Minnie allowed a logger access through her property. For a 155 acre parcel she paid one dollar. Other property was acquired through trade. However, if Minnie was ever boastful it was not over the millions of dollars in real estate she acquired. Even her best friend knew little of her land deals. What they likely would hear about were her flowers, garden, berries, and calves.

(6) Grandpa Oscar

There is no doubt Oscar was the laid back one, though with equal dexterity he could build a barn, move a house, replace a thrown horse shoe, calm a wild horse, fabricate a wagon part on his forge or spin a yarn. Minnie, on the other hand, was a planner and strategist. Oscar gambled on wildcat wells, dreamed of oil riches and accepted his luck graciously. Minnie gambled on horses, land and government contracts and didn't leave much to chance. Minnie at times got impatient with Oscar but was quick to get over it. Minnie never left Oscar for the mountains without a kiss.

118

(7) Grandma Minnie

There are those that are so young at heart they never seem to grow old. Minnie was so young at heart even the young did not think of her as old. For this reason, her friends spanned the generations. As she aged chronologically the young looked to her for guidance and the old for inspiration. Part of what attracted young people to Minnie was her love of games, checkers, cards, mumbly peg and any game that required skill with the element of chance. The games of strategy she loved the most. In later years she discovered the granddaddy of all games of strategy—chess. She played chess daily for years. When her eyesight got too bad to see the pieces, she got a bigger set and to play cards, bigger cards. Woe to those who underestimated Minnie's mental agility. They were invariably dealt a measure of humility along with their cards.

Life, of course, was the best game of all for Minnie, a game to be enjoyed and played with intensity and vigor.

(8) Minnie's choices

Minnie chose freedom over money, security, comfort and even, at times, friendship and family. She lived life on her terms. In the winter and spring she loved her husband and family. In the summer and fall she loved the Olympic Mountains. Minnie was never asked by her loved ones to choose between them and the high wild places she also loved.

Mr. Minnie Peterson?

APPENDIX

Letters from the Front -- WWI

Dec 2nd 1918

Dear Cousin,

I will answer your welcome letter which I received the other day was sure glad to hear from you all.

Well yes I certainly have been through some exciting adventures since I left there. The last place we were in was a hard battle out of Verdun we were up there when the armistice was signed and there was a happy bunch of fellows when all firing ceased. It was a great sight all along the front after the fighting was all over at night it was just like a big fourth of July fire works there was rockets of all kinds and flares lighting up the darkness all along the front, well it is all over now and I consider myself to be very lucky to come out safe.

I also received that picture you sent me but unfortunately I lost it in my rounds. I would be very thankful for the Christmas package you were speaking of but I think we will be on our way home shortly and I think it would be just as well not to send it across the water. As it is near supper time I will close for this time. Well I am well and feeling fine and hoping to find you all the same. Wishing you all a Merry Christmas and Happy New Year.

Your Cousin,
Emil Person
Is.E. 101. US Inf.
26 Div   Amer. E.F. France

Dec. 8, 1918

Dear Sister Minnie,

I received your letter last night and I am going to answer it at once. I am getting along fine and never felt any better in my life. Anyway. Minnie I have good news for you. I am pretty sure that we will start for home before the first of the year. You will see me drifting into Forks sometime in January or Feb.

I would have liked to have gone to Sweden but there is no chance of getting a discharge in France. I got a letter from Emil's brother and he wanted me to come over there but it is too late now as we have already received orders to return to the States. The climate is a lot better this winter than it was last winter. We are in a different place you know. Within a couple miles of the Swiss border. I think I will be home before Emil as he is in the Army that is going to the Rhine. He may not be home for three or four months.

from your brother,
William G. Nelson.
P.S. This will be the last letter that I will write.

Best friend's letters – the more things change

1211 Morton Ave.,
Pullman, Wn.

Jan. 23, 1916

Dear Minnie or must I call you Mrs. Peterson
All right then:

My Dear Mrs. Peterson:

I heard from Rudolph Dimmel that you were back and I couldn't wait any longer for you to write to me, so I had to write even if I don't know your address for sure.

I got your card when you were on your trip, I sure was glad to hear from an old friend again. I'll bet you had a good trip. My I wish I could have been with you. Did you get there in time to take in the fair? You'll have to write and tell me all about your trip.

Gee Minnie I mean Dickie, I wish you were back here again, I certainly have good times we go out skiing, coasting, and sleighing a whole bunch of us went to Moscow Friday night and came back by way of Clinton Grange. There was a dance there so we stopped and danced and got home at 4 o'clock. Last night I went to a skating party and had an awful good time. Oh gosh! Minnie can't you come over and visit me for awhile, I think your real mean to be as close as Spokane and not come down here. You went thru Spokane didn't you?

Well Minnie I don't know if you'll get this for I'm not sure where you are living now, so I'll close for this time hoping you'll answer me soon.

From an Old Friend of Yours,
Myrtle.

The people I'm staying with have a new born baby girl. Gee! It is the dearest baby and it's so good. I don't suppose you have any yet? Ha! Ha! Send Oscar my best regards and tell him to take good care of you. All I ask is that you answer with a few lines. Now that is not asking much is it?

616 So 15th
Tacoma, Wn

Mar 15, 1919
My Dear Minnie:

After giving up hopes of hearing from you the 23rd time made up my mind to write again. Of course I know you are very busy with the children and all but I think you could spare a moment once in a while to write. Are you coming to Tacoma and when? Be sure and let me know. For one of my summer trips, I guess I'll come up and see you Minnie. You see when you are working and making your own money, it isn't like if you have to ask Dad for it. So you see I am planning on some trips—and I'd like to see you as well as any one I know.

It sure is a typical spring day to-day. The sun is doing its best. Girls are popping out in spring coats and Easter bonnets. I'm going to be minus a spring coat if I have to pay 70 or $75 for one. I had my mind set on one and they only wanted $72.50 for it, all I said was good night coat and haven't tried another since.

How is your hubby and children. I hope it won't be long till I can see them and you in particular.

I was home again last week. You don't know how good it really is to spend even a day on the farm after a couple of weeks of city humdrum. I've been here over six months and the farm never seemed so good to me before. I have a mighty good position tho so I guess it's up to me to stay.

The 63rd Division arrived Thursday they sure had a mighty hearty welcome. Cars of all clubs and most of the Tacomans were down to meet them. Dances and parties and sightseeing cars were all in their honor. As far as I'm concerned I'd rather see them go ahead and get the boy a job rather than giving them dances, etc. But guess I'd better not start kicking in a letter so will leave that off.

Minnie did you ever eat real honest to goodness Chinese Noodles. Begin at one end and keep a going until you get to the other. Some sport to watch the other fellow. When you come to see me I sure am going to have you eat noodles. Really that pleases me more than a show. Especially if some one can use the chop sticks. As you can tell by my letter that news is scarce, I won't have to tell you that. Write to your devoted friend soon and often—with love to all, Myrtle

Oscar's Dream and Minnie's Reality

Forks, Wash.
Aug 19, 1928

Dear Oscar,
Well this is the evening after the night before, or at least I feel that away for I sure am sleepy.

Well Mr. Stay was down today and he wanted to see you the worst way so I told him it was impossible for you to come down so he told me to write this evening because he wants an answer right back from you as soon as he can. It seems that they can't get a reliable company to start work on oil claims. Therefore the claim holders have decided to raise enough money to build a road up river to claims. Stay said the contract calls for a road up there right away and since they can't get a company interested right now it is up to the holders to build it if they want to hold their claim. It will cost you $43 for your share, you will either have to do the work yourself or hire it done within the next month otherwise you will lose your claim. (and that would be just too bad) (Bull S.) Answer right away. So Mr. Stay will know if you want to hold your claim or not. Answer as soon as you get this letter. If a road is put up there then he is sure he can get a reliable company to work. $43 is about enough to buy another horse and a lot more use to us. But suit yourself if you want to hold it that is up to you. Only answer as soon as you get this letter as they are going to start work right away. Love,
Minnie

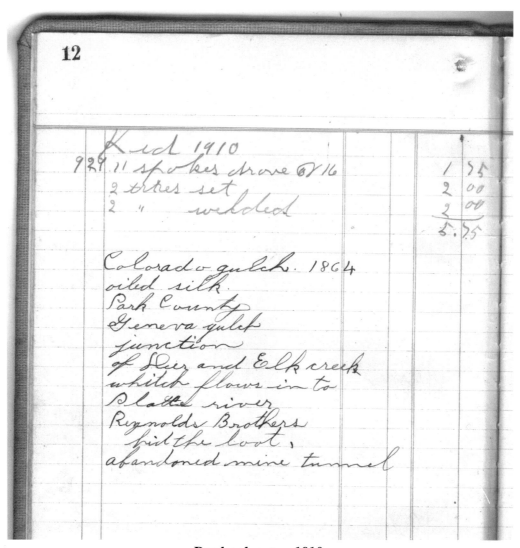

Day book entry -1910
Directions to a treasure

Forks, Wash.
Dec 7, 1932

Mr. R. O. Hom,
Spokane
Wash.   Dear Hom,

I am a long time answering your letters, but it was so late when I got them that we could not go. On the account of snow as this country is about 7000 ft high. I have all the confidence in the world in you and your rig, Every thing is just as I told you it was and sometimes this coming april, maybe about the last of april we can go. For the snow is on the ground down there untill about that time, and we would not want any one trailing us around on that part of a hunt,

If I don't starve to death in the mean time, things sure were plenty too.

The reason at I got Lue was that stuff, just had too sled in the spring on the fells untill about the first of November, But there was no money. But Hom we will maybe this I just know we will.

You write me some time about the first of april and we can arrange the trip then.

Yours sincerely,
Oscar A. Peterson
Forks

Plans for a treasure hunt

MAZAMAS

909 N.W. 19TH AVENUE
PORTLAND, OREGON 97209

COPY

September 6, 1966

Mr. Bennet T. Gale, Superintendent
Olympic National Park
600 Park Avenue
Port Angeles, Washington 98362   SUBJECT: Hoh River Trail Conditions

Dear Mr. Gale,

    I am writing you on Mazama letterhead so that you may know of my position as a Director of the Mazamas, but you should not construe this letter as representing the position of my club. Rather, it is a person to person effort to reach an understanding as to the trail conditions which are desirable for parties undertaking the climb of Mt. Olympus which I led for my club on August 29, 1966. I hope you will interpret this letter in the friendly way which it is intended.

    Every year, our club makes a climb of Mt. Olympus with a party of about twenty people. This year, we packed in 34 people plus a party of 17 which were to make a traverse of the Bailey Range.

    We engaged Mr. M.V. "Tex" Hutto, Box 412, Port Angeles, as our packer. About three quarters of a mile below Glacier Meadows, Mr. Hutto dropped our dunnage, declining to pack us the rest of the way into Glacier Meadows because THE TRAIL WAS NOT SAFE FOR HIS STOCK. Personally, I feel Mr. Hutto was entirely within his rights, and I have no complaint against him. He is a fine person and packer.

    However, this caused our party a delay of two hours in personally packing our dunnage the remaining distance to Glacier Meadows. In turn, this delay cost our party an attempt on the middle peak of Mt. Olympus although our party (including a girl of twelve) successfully climbed the west peak.

    Mr. Gale, I feel that there are a number of reasons for putting this trail in better shape - reasons which are more important than the disappointed personal feelings of the members of my party. These are:

    1) Because packing by horse in the Olympic National Park is a concession, parties are limited in their choice to a fixed number of packers. Trail conditions should be such that where one packer is able to go, another will be willing to go. Conditions should not be so marginal that only one packer will undertake the trip to Glacier Meadows. How is the public to know whom to contact?

Mr. Bennet T. Gale   September 6, 1966

        To my knowledge, Mrs. Oscar Peterson, Forks, Washington, is the only packer
currently willing to go the full distance into Glacier Meadows. I had the
opportunity to talk to her while in there and she, too, felt that trail conditions
were a great deal less than desirable.

        2) There is good forage for stock at Glacier Meadows. There is not any
forage at Elk Lake. This means that unless a packer can get through, he must
take his stock back down trail below the Hoh River Bridge on the same day he
packs in. Conversely, he must bring his stock up from below the bridge on the
same day he packs out. This added time can have a serious effect on the timetable,
not to mention the energies, of any parties contemplating a climb of Mt. Olympus.

        3) There is currently a great deal of discussion about the merits of a
North Cascade National Park. A number of opponents suggest that the creation of
this park will have serious adverse effects on the allocation of Park Service
funds for the maintenance of the Olympic National Park. Personally, I do not
see how their argument can be denied when the main trail to the mountain for
which the park is named is in such deplorable condition.

        According to the Trail Maintenance Supervisor at the Hoh River Ranger Station,
there is still time to put the trail in shap this fall, but he cannot do it alone.
I hope that you will see your way clear to authorize the necessary funds to make
the improvements needed in the last three quarters of a mile of an otherwise fine
trail.

        I am sending copies of this letter to those people whose interests are
vitally concerned with this trail and its users.

                                Sincerely,

                                James K. Angell

                                James K. Angell

cc. Mr. Edward Hummel, National Park Service, 450 Golden Gate Ave.
         Box 36063, San Francisco, Calif. 94102

     Head Ranger, Hoh River Ranger Station, Olympic National Park, Wash.

     Mr. Carmie Dafoe, Chairman, Mazama Climbing Committee,
         909 N.W. 19th Ave., Portland, Oregon 97210

     Mr. Al Combs, Sierra Club, P.O. Box 3941, Portland, Oregon 97208

     Mr. M.V. "Tex" Hutto, Box 412, Port Angeles, Wash.

     Mrs. Oscar Peterson, Sr., Forks, Wash.

Jackson Ranger Station add-on under construction - 1920's.
Charlie Lewis on left, Sanford Floe on right
Courtesy of Marilyn Lewis

Jackson Ranger Station - 1950's

Olympus Guard Station, Lewis Meadow - 1920's

Olympus Guard Station - 1920's
Courtesy of U.S. Forest Service

The Boys of Summer - Rangers and Fire Guards - late thirties
Left to right, standing - Floyd Dickinson, Wally Gittings, John Robinson, Wally Edwards
kneeling - Jim Byrne, Manard Fields
Courtesy of Olympic National Park

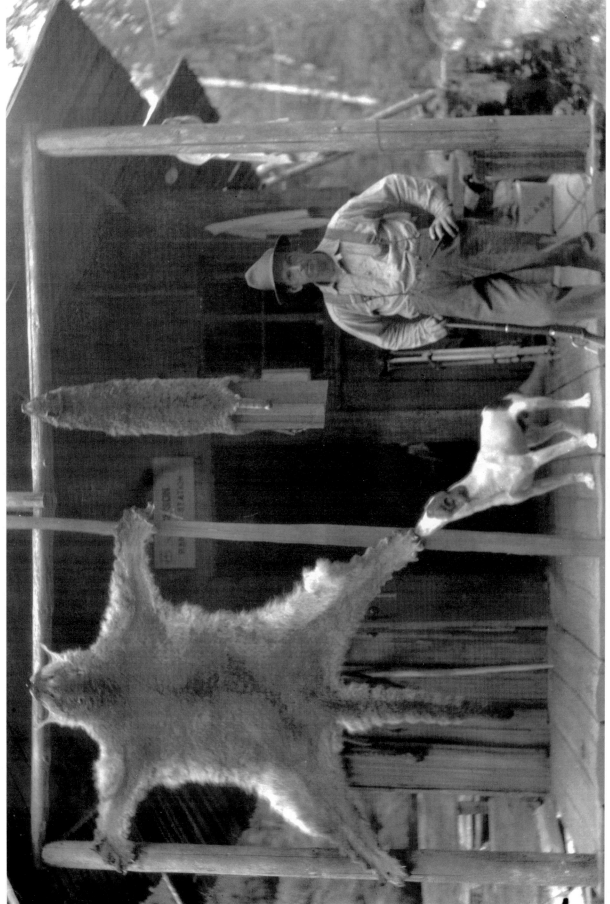

Bogachiel Guard Station - 1920's

Lake Creek Guard Station below Hoh Lake - 1920's

Minnie and friends, Micky Merchant in back - late forties

Minnie and client. Background - Sol Duc Valley, mid thirties.

Claude Clark and Oscar (Pete) at the terminus of Blue Glacier - 1939.

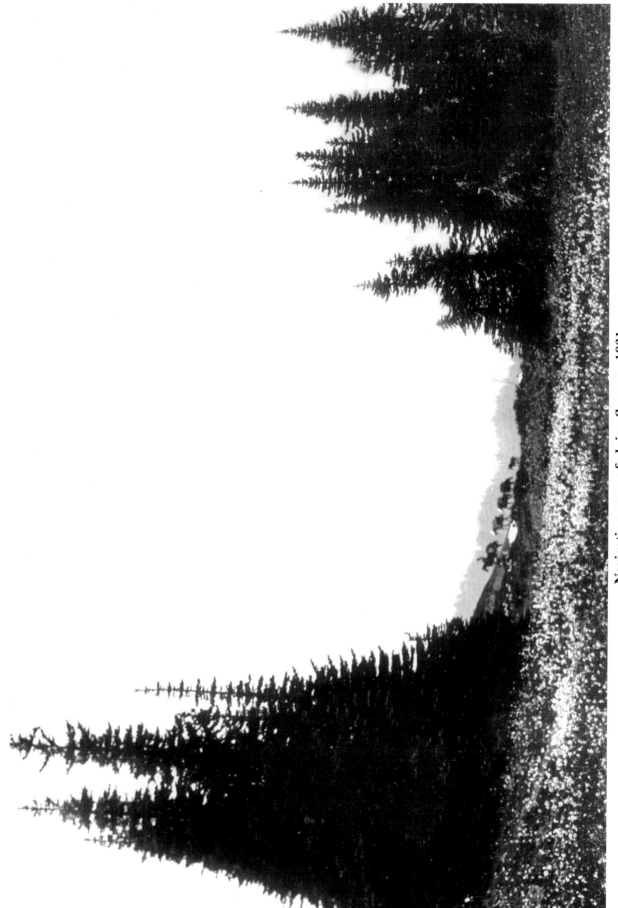

Navigating a sea of alpine flowers - 1931
Hibben and Bole photo

BIBLIOGRAPHY

Archibald, Lonnie. *There Was a Day: Stories of the Pioneers.* Forks, WA: Olympic Graphic Arts 1999.

Arnold, William. *Shadowland.* New York: Berkley Books 1978.

Back, Joe. *Horses, Hitches, and Rocky Trails.* Boulder, CO: Johnson Books 1987.

Bird, Rebecca. "Minnie Peterson: Packing them in for fifty years." *Passages:Northwest Orient In flight Magazine* March 1973.

Bragg, L.E. *Myths and Mysteries of Washington.* Guilford, CT: Globe Pequot Press 2005.

Daly, Dorothy. "Days before the little red school house." *Seattle Post Intelligencer: Sunday Pictorial Review* 14 July 1963.

Fletcher, Elizabeth. *The Iron Man of the Hoh.* Port Angeles, WA: Creative Communications 1979.

Green, Ranny. "Mighty Minnie's Going Strong." *Seattle Times: Pacific Magazine* 9 May 1982.

Hazard, Joseph T. *Snow Sentinels of the Pacific Northwest.* Seattle: Lowman and Hanford, 1932.

Hillinger, Charles. "Suddenly Last Summer-Life in a Rainforest." *Los Angeles Times* Sept. 1985.

Horswill, Emily. "Minnie and the Mountains." *Backpacking Journal* Fall 1977:Vol.3 No. 3.

Horswill, Emily. "Minnie Peterson-Living Legend in the Olympics." *Signpost for Northwest Hikers* May 1978.

Howell, Erle. "Saleswoman for the Olympics." *Seattle Times* 9 Oct. 1949.

Hult, Ruby. *Untamed Olympics: The Story of a Peninsula.* Portland, OR: Binfords & Mort 1956.

"Joe Jeffers, Tragedy and Legacy." *Straight History: Historical Quarterly of the Clallam County Historical Museum* Autumn 1989 Vol. 5 No. 1.

Jordan, Teresa. *Cowgirls: Women of the American West.* Lincoln: University of Nebraska Press 1992.

Kirk, Ruth. "Minnie Peterson-Olympics Packer." *Seattle Times: Pictorial Magazine*
    May 1968.

Kirk, Ruth. "The Hoh." *Seattle Times: Sunday Pictorial* 25 Nov. 1962.

McDonald, Lucile. "Forks prepares for another glorious 4th." *Seattle Times Magazine*
    9 June 1960.

Miletich, Phyliss. "Meet Minnie: Lady Horsepacker of the Olympics." *Peninsula
    Magazine* Spring/Summer 1986.

Morgan, Murray. *The Last Wilderness*. Seattle: University of Washington Press 1997.

Morgenroth, Chris. *Footprints in the Olympics: An Autobiography*. Fairfield, WA: Ye
    Galleon Press 1991.

Muller, Will. "Minnie the Packer." *Western Horseman* Dec. 1975.

Newlan, Bobbe. "Minnie Peterson: Mountains are her world." *Port Angeles Evening
    News* 26 June 1967, Fourth of July edition.

Rooney, J.R. *Frontier Legacy*. Seattle:Northwest Interpretive Association 1997.

Smith, LeRoy. *Pioneers of the Olympic Peninsula*. Forks, WA: Olympic Graphic Arts
    1977.

"Women at Work." *Working Woman*. Oct. 1979.

Wood, Robert. *Across the Olympic Mountains*. Seattle: The Mountaineers and
    University of Washington Press 1967.

Wood, Robert. *Olympic Mountains Trail Guide*. Seattle: The Mountaineers 1991.

INDEX

136

About the authors:

Gary Peterson and Glynda Peterson Schaad are fifth generation natives of the Olympic Peninsula. Gary holds an undergraduate degree in mathematics from Seattle Pacific University and a graduate degree in math from the University of Idaho. He also studied at the University of Washington and the University of Vienna-Austria. He has taught math and worked for the US Forest Service. Presently Gary manages family property in the Hoh River Valley where he lives with his wife, Charlotte.

Glynda graduated from Seattle Pacific University with an English degree. She received a Masters in English from the University of Washington and currently teaches at Peninsula College in Port Angeles, WA. Glynda spent many summers working for Minnie on her Hoh ranch.